James M. Buchanan

Series Introduction

The *Major Conservative and Libertarian Thinkers* series aims to show that there is a rigorous, scholarly tradition of social and political thought that may be broadly described as 'conservative', 'libertarian' or some combination of the two.

The series aims to show that conservatism is not simply a reaction against contemporary events, nor a privileging of intuitive thought over deductive reasoning; libertarianism is not simply an apology for unfettered capitalism or an attempt to justify a misguided atomistic concept of the individual. Rather, the thinkers in this series have developed coherent intellectual positions that are grounded in empirical reality and also founded upon serious philosophical reflection on the relationship between the individual and society, how the social institutions necessary for a free society are to be established and maintained, and the implications of the limits to human knowledge and certainty.

Each volume in the series presents a thinker's ideas in an accessible and cogent manner to provide an indispensable work for students with varying degrees of familiarity with the topic as well as more advanced scholars.

The following twenty volumes that make up the entire *Major Conservative and Libertarian Thinkers* series are written by international scholars and experts:

The Salamanca School by Andre Azevedo Alves (LSE, UK) and
    José Manuel Moreira (Universidade de Aveiro, Portugal)
Thomas Hobbes by R. E. R. Bunce (Cambridge, UK)
John Locke by Eric Mack (Tulane, UK)
David Hume by Christopher J. Berry (Glasgow, UK)
Adam Smith by James Otteson (Yeshiva, US)
Edmund Burke by Dennis O'Keeffe (Buckingham, UK)
Alexis de Tocqueville by Alan S Kahan (Paris, France)
Herbert Spencer by Alberto Mingardi (Istituto Bruno Leoni, Italy)
Ludwig von Mises by Richard Ebeling (Northwood, US)

Joseph A. Schumpeter by John Medearis (Riverside, California, US)
F. A. Hayek by Adam Tebble (UCL, UK)
Michael Oakeshott by Edmund Neill (Oxford, UK)
Karl Popper by Phil Parvin (Loughborough, UK)
Ayn Rand by Mimi Gladstein (Texas, US)
Milton Friedman by William Ruger (Texas State, US)
Russell Kirk by John Pafford (Northwood, US)
James M. Buchanan by John Meadowcroft (King's College London, UK)
The Modern Papacy by Samuel Gregg (Acton Institute, US)
Murray Rothbard by Gerard Casey (UCD, Ireland)
Robert Nozick by Ralf Bader (St Andrews, UK)

Of course, in any series of this nature, choices have to be made as to which thinkers to include and which to leave out. Two of the thinkers in the series – F. A. Hayek and James M. Buchanan – have written explicit statements rejecting the label 'conservative'. Similarly, other thinkers, such as David Hume and Karl Popper, may be more accurately described as classical liberals than either conservatives or libertarians. But these thinkers have been included because a full appreciation of this particular tradition of thought would be impossible without their inclusion; conservative and libertarian thought cannot be fully understood without some knowledge of the intellectual contributions of Hume, Hayek, Popper and Buchanan, among others. While no list of conservative and libertarian thinkers can be perfect, then, it is hoped that the volumes in this series come as close as possible to providing a comprehensive account of the key contributors to this particular tradition.

John Meadowcroft
King's College London

James M. Buchanan

John Meadowcroft

Major Conservative and Libertarian Thinkers

Series Editor: John Meadowcroft

BLOOMSBURY
NEW YORK · LONDON · NEW DELHI · SYDNEY

Bloomsbury Academic
An imprint of Bloomsbury Publishing Plc

1385 Broadway	50 Bedford Square
New York	London
NY 10018	WC1B 3DP
USA	UK

www.bloomsbury.com

Hardback edition first published in 2011 by the Continuum International Publishing Group Inc.

This paperback edition published by Bloomsbury Academic 2013

© John Meadowcroft, 2013

All rights reserved. No part of this publication may be reproduced or transmitted in any form or by any means, electronic or mechanical, including photocopying, recording, or any information storage or retrieval system, without prior permission in writing from the publishers.

No responsibility for loss caused to any individual or organization acting on or refraining from action as a result of the material in this publication can be accepted by Bloomsbury Academic or the author.

Library of Congress Cataloging-in-Publication Data
A catalog record for this book is available from the Library of Congress.

ISBN: HB: 978-0-8264-3080-9
PB: 978-1-4411-9575-3
ePub: 978-1-6235-6710-1

Typeset by Newgen Imaging Systems Pvt Ltd, Chennai, India

Contents

Acknowledgements ix
The Referencing of Buchanan's Work in this Book xi

1. Buchanan's Intellectual Biography 1
   Introduction 1
   Early Years and War Years 4
   Chicago 7
      Frank Knight 8
      Knut Wicksell 11
   Knoxville, Tallahassee and the Italian Year 16
   Virginia Political Economy 19
      Charlottesville 20
      UCLA and 'academia in anarchy' 24
      Blacksburg 27
      Fairfax 31
   Nobel Prize and Beyond 32

2. Buchanan's Ideas 35
   Introduction 35
   The Individualist Postulate 37
   The Problems of Anarchy 45
   Rights 50
   Political Agreement and Constitutional Choice:
      Enter the State 52
   Public Goods, the Productive State and
      Non-Unanimous Decisions 56

Constitutional Democracy: Procedural
not Substantive   60
The Problems of Non-Contractarian Politics:
Re-Entering Anarchy   63
Individual preferences and 'democratic' outcomes   65
Exploitation or the imposition of external costs   82
Rent-seeking   92
The state: the threat of Leviathan   96
Constitutionalism: Solving the Problems
of Politics   107
A fiscal constitution   110
Qualified majority decision-making   119
Federalism   121
Constitutional revolution   123
Conclusion   129

3. **The Reception and Influence of Buchanan's Work**   133
Introduction   133
The Intellectual Impact and Influence
of Public Choice Theory   134
The Critics of Buchanan and Public
Choice Theory   140
Methodological individualism   141
Self-interest   145
Rationality   149
Unanimity   151
Power   155
The Development of Public Choice as
an Academic Community   157

4. **The Continuing and Future Relevance
of Buchanan's Ideas**   161

Bibliography   166
Index   171

Acknowledgements

As the editor of the series in which this book appears I would like to begin by expressing my thanks to Marie-Claire Antoine of Bloomsbury for her brilliant work in helping to bring the series to publication. I would also like to thank Anthony Haynes, the original commissioning editor of the series at Continuum, for inviting me to be series editor. Thanks are also due to the other nineteen authors for writing such excellent books within a strict timescale to enable the publication of twenty books in two years.

In respect of the present book, I would like to André Azevedo Alves for reading the second chapter and providing extremely helpful and detailed comments and feedback. Over the last few years I have had many conversations about Buchanan, public choice theory and political economy more generally with Anthony J. Evans, Paul Lewis and Mark Pennington that have undoubtedly contributed to the development of this work. Also, I would like to acknowledge the support of my colleagues in the Department of Political Economy at King's College London, most notably Professor Ken Young, in my academic endeavours.

I was fortunate to be the only author in this series able to send their book to the subject on publication. Professor Buchanan was good enough to read the book and to point out a small number of factual errors that have been corrected in this paperback edition. I have also corrected two factual errors identified in Randall G. Holcombe's review of the hardback edition in the journal *Public Choice*. I have also clarified the argumentation in one or two places in light of comments made by a referee for *Public Choice* on an article submitted to the journal that drew upon some of the material herein. I would like to thank all three individuals for their comments and the publishers Continuum for making these changes.

Sadly, Professor Buchanan died on 9 January 2013. I hope this book can contribute in some small way to the preservation and extension of the influence of his remarkable lifetime of scholarship.

John Meadowcroft
King's College London

The Referencing of Buchanan's Work in this Book

Throughout this book references to Buchanan's own work included in his Collected Works published by Liberty Fund of Indianapolis between 1998 and 2003 are to the versions of his works that appear in those volumes. It has been decided to reference the Liberty Fund editions on the presumption that in the future these editions will become the standard versions of Buchanan's works. The following abbreviations have been used in the text:

LFCL: Volume 1, *The Logical Foundations of Constitutional Liberty* (collected articles and papers)

PPPD: Volume 2, *Public Principles of Public Debt* (book, originally published in 1958)

CoC: Volume 3, *The Calculus of Consent* (book, originally published in 1962, co-authored with Gordon Tullock)

PFDP: Volume 4, *Public Finance in Democratic Process* (book, originally published in 1967)

DSPG: Volume 5, *The Demand and Supply of Public Goods* (book, originally published in 1968)

CaC: Volume 6, *Cost and Choice* (book, originally published in 1969)

LoL: Volume 7, *The Limits of Liberty* (book, originally published in 1975)
DiD: Volume 8, *Democracy in Deficit* (book, originally published in 1977, co-authored with Richard E. Wagner)
PT: Volume 9, *The Power to Tax* (book, originally published in 1980, co-authored with Geoffrey Brennan)
RoR: Volume 10, *The Reason of Rules* (book, originally published in 1985, co-authored with Geoffrey Brennan)
PPNI: Volume 11, *Politics by Principle, Not Interest* (book, originally published in 1998, co-authored with Roger D. Congleton)
EIIL: Volume 12, *Economic Inquiry and Its Logic* (collected articles and papers)
PPC: Volume 13, *Politics as Public Choice* (collected articles and papers)
DT: Volume 14, *Debt and Taxes* (collected articles and papers)
EPET: Volume 15, *Externalities and Public Expenditure Theory* (collected articles and papers)
CCC: Volume 16, *Choice, Contract and Constitutions* (collected articles and papers)
MSMO: Volume 17, *Moral Science and Moral Order* (collected articles and papers)
FLL: Volume 18, *Federalism, Liberty, and the Law* (collected articles and papers)
IPE: Volume 19, *Ideas, Persons and Events* (collected articles and papers)

The twentieth volume contains an index to the entire Collected Works.

Three of Buchanan's books do not appear in the Collected Works. The following abbreviations are used in the text to refer to these books:

AiA: *Academia in Anarchy,* New York: Basic Books, 1970, co-authored with Nicos D. Devletoglou

WITANAC: *Why I, Too, Am Not a Conservative,* Cheltenham, UK: Edward Elgar, 2004

EFTOI: *Economics from the Outside In,* College Station, TX: Texas A&M Press, 2007

In addition, a 1999 book in which Buchanan and Richard A. Musgrave engaged in a debate about questions of public finance and public choice was also not included in Buchanan's collected works. This book is abbreviated as follows:

PFPC: *Public Finance and Public Choice,* with Richard A. Musgrave, Cambridge, MA: MIT Press, 1999.

Finally, Buchanan published with a number of co-authors during his career. Throughout this book it is assumed that the co-published works represent Buchanan's own personal views, unless there is a reason not to do so, such as where authorship of specific chapters is assigned to the different co-authors, or where there are known differences of opinion between the authors on particular issues.

Chapter 1

Buchanan's Intellectual Biography

Introduction

On 16 October 1986 the Royal Swedish Academy of Sciences announced the award of the 1986 Alfred Nobel Memorial Prize in Economic Sciences to Professor James McGill Buchanan 'for his development of the contractual and constitutional bases for the theory of economic and political decision-making' (Nobel Prize Citation, in LFCL, p. 3).

The award of the Nobel Prize in economics – the most prestigious professional accolade that can be presented to an economist – to Buchanan was first and foremost recognition of the importance of his personal contributions to the discipline of economics. Whereas mainstream, neo-classical economics focuses on private decisions in markets, Buchanan's work was groundbreaking in applying economic theory and analysis to public decisions in the political realm: public choice. The award of the Nobel Prize to Buchanan also recognized the importance of the scholarly contribution made more generally by public choice theory, the new political economy that Buchanan had helped to establish as a powerful intellectual force in the social sciences.

Political economy involves comparative analysis of politics and markets as institutions via which people seek to achieve individual and collective ends. It would seem logical, therefore, for economists to apply the same basic analytical framework to investigate the political realm as that employed to understand the economic realm. Yet, surely surprisingly, economic analysis had not been applied to the political realm in any systematic way before the work of Buchanan and the early pioneers of public choice theory. Hence, Buchanan later wrote of what is now considered a classic 1954 article comparing individual choice in voting and the market that 'the points made seemed simple, but surprisingly no one had made such a basic comparison' (LFCL, p. 16). Similarly, when Buchanan and co-author Gordon Tullock wrote what may now be considered the foundational text of public choice theory, *The Calculus of Consent*, it was not with the sense that they were discovering new frontiers, but rather with the feeling that they were working through a series of seemingly straightforward applications of economic theory:

> Tullock and I considered ourselves to be applying relatively simple economic analysis to the choice among alternative political decision rules, with more or less predictable results. We realized that no one had attempted to do precisely what we were doing, but the exercise was essentially one of 'writing up the obvious' rather than opening up wholly new areas for inquiry. (LFCL, p. 19)

Although the basic premise of public choice theory that economic analysis can be usefully applied to the study of non-market decision-making may seem relatively obvious and imply a relatively straightforward research agenda, the results that follow have often been highly controversial.

In particular, public choice theory logically leads to questions about the efficacy and therefore desirability of political decision-making relative to the choices people make in markets. For example, in the political realm voters are required to choose every four or five years between a small number of large bundles of goods and services offered by different parties or candidates, often constituting between a third and a half of GDP, whereas in the marketplace people may purchase relatively discrete, personal bundles of goods and services on a day-by-day basis. On this basis it may be concluded that choices made in the marketplace are more likely to correspond to individual preferences than choices made in the political realm (LFCL, pp. 81–82; PFDP, Chapter 6). It is conclusions like this that imply criticism of democratic institutions and practices that many scholars have found difficult to accept (e.g. Kelman, 1988; Self, 1993; Shapiro, 1996; Udehn, 1996, pp. 180–184).

Buchanan's ideas will be discussed in detail in Chapter 2, and the key criticisms of his ideas will be considered in Chapter 3. This chapter will provide an intellectual biography of Buchanan that sets out the key life events and experiences that influenced his scholarly work. After this introduction, the next section will set out Buchanan's early life in rural Tennessee, early academic training and his war service. The third section will present Buchanan's entry to the University of Chicago where he encountered the two most important scholarly influences on his life: his teacher Frank Knight and the hitherto neglected work of the Swedish economist Knut Wicksell. The fourth section will then give an account of Buchanan's early academic appointments and his encounters with Italian public finance theorists during a year spent in Italy in the early part of his career. The fifth section will set out the historical development of Buchanan's contribution to public choice theory against the backdrop of dramatic social change and social unrest in the United States and in the context of the creation of a series of institutional centres for public choice scholarship in the State of Virginia, that led Buchanan's particular brand of public choice that emphasizes the importance of institutions to political outcomes to be named Virginia public choice theory. A short final section will bring the account up to date with consideration of Buchanan's life after the award of the Nobel Prize.

Early Years and War Years

In an essay written less than two years after his receipt of the Nobel Prize, Buchanan wrote that 'if Jim Buchanan can get a Nobel Prize, anyone can' (EFTOI, p. 35). What Buchanan meant by this statement was that if someone from his relatively humble background who had spent his teaching and research career at provincial university institutions could achieve such an accolade, then anyone could do the same:

> Here was Jim Buchanan, a country boy from Middle Tennessee, educated in rural public schools and a local public teachers college, who is not associated with an establishment university, who has never shared the academically fashionable soft left ideology, who has worked in totally unorthodox subject matter with very old-fashioned tools of analysis, chosen by a distinguished and respected Swedish committee. (EFTOI, p. 36)

Buchanan, then, was not born into privilege, nor did he live and work in the most rarefied academic settings. His work challenged the prevailing ideological current of his time, yet he was able to achieve the highest possible academic recognition.

James M. Buchanan was born on 3 October 1919 in Murfreesboro, a small town in the largely rural Southern US state of Tennessee. His family owned a small farm, on which Buchanan was born and grew up. Buchanan later wrote that 'My family was poor, but, in the county, it was important' (LFCL, p. 11). This importance came from the fact that Buchanan's grandfather, John P. Buchanan, had been a governor of the State of Tennessee as a representative of the populist Farmers' Alliance Party from 1891 to 1893. Buchanan attended the local public school, named Buchanan School, in tribute to his grandfather.

Buchanan has written that his parents had high hopes that he would emulate his grandfather's success in the world of politics, via training in law at the prestigious Vanderbilt University in the state capital of Nashville. However, 'Economic reality destroyed this dream', as the depression meant that Buchanan could only afford to attend Middle Tennessee Teachers College in Murfreesboro. Buchanan enrolled in 1936 and lived at home on the family farm which enabled him to pay for fees and books 'by milking dairy cows morning and night for four years' (LFCL, p. 12). The disappointment of not being able to attend a premier university, combined with missing out on the quality of tuition available at Vanderbilt, could have been an overwhelming setback, but Buchanan has written positively of the enduring impact of the intellectual and personal education he received from committed and talented teachers at Middle Tennessee Teachers College. In particular, Buchanan received a sound basic college education with a strong grounding in mathematics and statistics (EFTOI, Chapter 3).

Buchanan left Murfreesboro in 1940 to take up a $50 per month graduate fellowship in economics at the University of Tennessee at Knoxville. This choice did not represent any burning desire on Buchanan's part at that time to become a professional economist, but rather a more general preference for paid further study over entry into the world of work. Buchanan's time at Knoxville was socially, though not academically, rewarding: 'I learned no economics during that year, but I did learn about women and whiskey, which, after all, are important parts of an education' (LFCL, p. 13).

Plans that Buchanan made for further graduate studies were interrupted when he was drafted into the US Navy in August 1941. Buchanan had what he later described as an 'easy war', based at US fleet headquarters in Pearl Harbor and at Guam organizing the supply of the US ships engaged in the Pacific campaign. Buchanan's only involvement in the shooting war was a six-week tour at sea during one of the Pacific island invasions where he was 'close in enough to hear the guns and see the fires' (EFTOI, p. 59). Buchanan considered his four years in the navy as an important chapter in his education, sometimes in ways that were not intended by the naval staff. One event in particular contributed to Buchanan's lasting sense of being outside of the established elite. Within the navy, recruits were divided into companies, platoons and sections, each led by commanding officers. Graduates from Ivy League universities were automatically appointed to the officer positions on the basis of their Ivy League background. While Buchanan accepted that there may be some statistical probability that graduates of such institutions might be intellectually superior to other recruits, he nevertheless felt that this was 'blatant discrimination ... against southerners, mid-westerners, and westerners'. The perceived unfairness of this experience left a lasting mark on Buchanan, such that he later wrote: 'From that day forward, I have shared in the emotional damage imposed by discrimination, in any form, and "fairness" assumed for me a central normative position decades before I came to discuss principles of justice professionally and philosophically' (EFTOI, p. 49–50).

At the end of the war Buchanan was encouraged by his senior officers to consider a career in the navy. Buchanan had been awarded a Bronze Star for distinguished service, the navy had become his life and he 'had met all of the very important senior officers, along with many who would become important in the years ahead'. The alternative to a naval career was to return to graduate studies with a view to earning his PhD and becoming an academic. Buchanan later recalled that the 'choice was not an easy one', but he opted for academia in large part because he believed that as a reserve officer from a Southern background with little experience at sea he would always face 'some residual prejudice' likely to slow or stall his progress through the ranks of the navy (EFTOI, p. 66).

Chicago

In October 1945 Buchanan married Ann Bakke, whom he had met during his war service, in San Francisco. They would remain together for the rest of their lives. Equipped with a GI grant and a fellowship from the Southern Regional Training Program in Public Administration, Buchanan enrolled in the doctoral economics programme at the University of Chicago. Buchanan chose Chicago on the advice of C. C. Sims, a political science tutor at Middle

Tennessee Teachers College, who had described to Buchanan the intellectual ferment of the University of Chicago. This was a decision that Buchanan never regretted. Some 40 years later he commented: 'In retrospect I could not have made a better selection. Sims was precisely on target in conveying the intellectual excitement of the University of Chicago' (IPE, p. 6).

Frank Knight

Buchanan entered the University of Chicago with strong socialist beliefs. His undergraduate education in Tennessee and his postgraduate year in economics at Knoxville had contained no account of the workings or benefits of a market economy, so that, in Buchanan's words: 'I remained blissfully ignorant of the coordinating properties of a decentralized market process, an ignorance that made me vulnerable to quasi-Marxist arguments and explanations about economic history and economic reality' (IPE, p. 5). Buchanan's leftist leanings had been further heightened by his experience of discrimination in the navy, so much so that Buchanan later told one interviewer that this experience had – at that time – 'made me into a flaming communist. I would have signed up immediately to the Communist Party had a recruiter come along' (Horn, 2009, p. 95).

Buchanan's socialist leanings, however, were straightened by his exposure at Chicago to the tuition of Frank Knight:

> At Chicago, I found myself no different from my graduate-student colleagues, almost all of whom were socialist of one or another stripe. But within six weeks after enrolment in Frank Knight's course in price theory, I had

been converted into a zealous advocate of the market order. (LFCL, p. 15)

Although the Chicago economics department of the 1940s contained a glittering array of intellectual talent, including such world-renowned figures as Jacob Viner and Milton Friedman, there was no doubt in Buchanan's mind that Frank Knight was the dominant intellectual figure among the economics faculty at that time (IPE, p. 77).

Frank H. Knight (1885–1972) was one of the founders of modern neoclassical economics. His PhD dissertation, published in 1921 as *Risk, Uncertainty and Profit*, had established the distinction between rent, which was the legitimate return on a distributive share, and profit, which results from successful decision-making in the context of uncertainty. Knight had been appointed Professor of Economics at Chicago in 1927 and, along with Jacob Viner, he effectively founded the Chicago School of Economics, probably the most important school in neoclassical economic scholarship.

As Boyd (1997) has observed, however, Knight was also a paradoxical figure. Although one of the founders of neoclassical economics and thus an individual with a deep appreciation of the workings of a market economy, Knight was also one of the most searching critics of the assumptions of neoclassical economics and the market order. Hence, 'while at moments Knight prominently defended human freedom and the liberal order, at other times he was sufficiently moved by the shortcomings of liberalism as to condemn liberal society as "sick"' (Boyd, 1997, p. vii). Knight believed, then, that the role of social science scholarship was to draw out the paradoxes and ambiguities in human affairs, rather than to construct models that assumed away such complexities and tensions.

Like Buchanan, Knight was from a poor rural background and had been educated in Tennessee; in this sense Knight was also something of an outsider within an American academy that was felt to be dominated by an Ivy League elite. Their shared Southern heritage was probably a reason why Buchanan and Knight established a friendship that continued long after Buchanan left Chicago. As Buchanan later reflected: 'These common threads of experience established a relationship that I shared with no other professor' (IPE, p. 11; See also: IPE, pp. 77–85).

In intellectual terms, Buchanan learned two important lessons from Knight. First, as noted above, from Knight's classes in price theory Buchanan gained an appreciation of the operation of private markets that was to remain with him for the rest of his life. He later wrote: 'I had been converted into a strong advocacy of the market organization of the economy . . . through a mere six-week exposure to Frank Knight', via which, 'I became a born-again free-market advocate' (IPE, pp. 165–166). Buchanan's exposure to an effective account of how a market economy driven by the price mechanism spontaneously created social order converted him from socialist sympathizer to committed free marketeer once and for all. This understanding of the operation of a market economy would be central to all of Buchanan's later scholarship.

Second, Buchanan learned from Knight that in terms of academic inquiry 'nothing was sacrosanct, not the dogmas of religion, not the laws and institutions of social order, not the prevailing moral norms, not the accepted interpretations of sacred or profane texts' (IPE, p. 77). According to Knight's perspective, there could be no exemptions from scholarly analysis. Rather, 'Anything and everything was a potential subject for critical scrutiny, with an evaluative judgment to be informed by, but ultimately made independent of, external influence' (IPE, p. 78). Buchanan took from Knight the idea that scholars should bring their critical intelligence to bear on whatever institutions or ideas their work demanded. The advance of knowledge, and hence human progress, required that no areas be placed beyond the scope of critical inquiry. In Buchanan's work this approach can be seen most clearly in his unflinching and unromantic analysis of the workings of democracy; the notion that democracy is a principle that is in some way beyond criticism is entirely absent from Buchanan's analysis.

Knut Wicksell

The second critical influence that Buchanan encountered at the University of Chicago was the Swedish economist Knut Wicksell. But whereas Buchanan had direct contact with Frank Knight in the classroom, he encountered Wicksell only via his works in the university library.

Knut Wicksell (1851–1926) might be uncharitably described as an obscure Swedish economist. He held a chair in economics at the University of Lund in the early years of the twentieth century and made important contributions to the economic theory of interest, money and capital, as well as participating in public debates on questions of political economy in Sweden. Much of Wicksell's work was published in Swedish and German and not translated into English until after his death, if it all, making his contributions inaccessible to those without sufficient command of these two languages.

In the summer of 1948, soon after he had submitted his doctoral thesis, Buchanan happened to pull a copy of a work in German by Wicksell from the shelves of Chicago's Harper Library. It was titled *Finanztheoretische Untersuchungen*, had been published in 1896, and was, in Buchanan's words, 'a book that was untranslated and unknown' (LFCL, p. 15). Buchanan had sufficient knowledge of German to read it and later recalled: 'The effect on me was dramatic. Wicksell laid out before me a set of ideas that seemed to correspond precisely with those that I had already in my head, ideas that I could not express and would not have dared to express in the public-finance mind-set of the time' (LFCL, p. 15).

Wicksell's central thesis was a critique of the public finance orthodoxy that the relevant evaluative criterion for public expenditure proposals was whether the anticipated benefits to society exceeded the expected costs. Wicksell identified two fundamental problems with this orthodox approach. First, the evaluation of costs and benefits to society raised the epistemological question of how those costs and benefits were to be identified and quantified. Here, Wicksell took a methodological individualist approach, viewing society as simply an amalgam of the different individuals who composed that society. Accordingly, the costs and benefits to society of any public expenditure proposal was simply the sum of the benefits and costs for each individual. But for each individual, calculating those costs and benefits in advance would prove extremely difficult:

> [I]t is often very difficult for the individual to judge to what extent a proposed expansion of a certain state operation ... would provide him or those whose interests concern him most closely, with benefits corresponding to the sacrifice of having to pay a given amount of new taxes. (Wicksell, 1994, p. 79)

If it was difficult for any one individual to judge the personal costs and benefits of a public expenditure proposal, then it would be near impossible for another individual to make such a judgement on behalf of countless other people: 'If the individual is unable to form even an approximately definite judgement on this point, it is *a fortiori* impossible for anyone, even if he be a statesman of genius, to weigh the whole community's utility and sacrifice against each other' (p. 79). Wicksell argued, then, that the notion that benevolent legislators or bureaucrats could evaluate public expenditure proposals on the basis of whether the benefits accrued to society exceeded the costs implied the existence of omniscient decision-makers who did not in fact exist.

The second fallacy of the orthodox approach to public finance that Wicksell identified was the principle that the legislature 'must approve every state service and every public expenditure which imposes upon the community a sacrifice which is smaller than the expected usefulness and hence the value of the service to the community' (Wicksell, 1994, p. 76).

Wicksell contended that the principle that public expenditure proposals alleged or proven to produce net benefits should be approved did not take into account the distribution of those costs and benefits between different individuals and groups within society. Hence, any public expenditure proposal that had the effect of redistributing income from a minority to the majority, or from a smaller group to a larger group, would by definition meet the criterion of net community benefit. For Wicksell, such a situation was contrary to basic principles of justice and fairness: 'It would seem to be a blatant injustice if someone should be forced to contribute toward the costs of some activity which does not further his interests or may even be diametrically opposed to them' (p. 89). Wicksell argued that this seemingly innocuous principle of public finance was in fact a manifesto for coercion and exploitation via the political process.

Wicksell proposed a radical solution to the problems of orthodox public finance theory that he had identified.

Wicksell argued that decisions in matters of public expenditure should be taken on the basis of voluntary consent and hence unanimity. If a public expenditure proposal did indeed produce benefits that exceeded its costs, then it must logically be possible to distribute those benefits and costs so that every individual gained. In such a situation, unanimous approval of the proposed expenditure would be entirely plausible. For Wicksell, the application of the principle of unanimity was the only way to ensure that the power of the state to levy taxation did not become a means of legal exploitation: 'In the final analysis, unanimity and fully voluntary consent in the making of decisions provide the only certain and palpable guarantee against injustice in tax distribution' (p. 91).

Wicksell accepted that an absolute rule of unanimity was impractical, so instead proposed the use of different qualified majority voting rules to approve different magnitudes of public expenditure. Wicksell's proposal, then, was for the adoption of a fiscal constitution to set binding decision-making rules to ensure that public expenditure proposals commanded the consent of those who were required to pay for them. This, Wicksell argued, was the only way to ensure just taxation.

For those already familiar with Buchanan's work and/or public choice theory more generally, the similarities with Wicksell's theory of just taxation and the public choice approach will be immediately apparent. As Reisman (1990, p. 4) noted, 'No person who reads Wicksell having read Buchanan can fail to be impressed by the similarities between the two authors'. Indeed, in the lecture delivered on the occasion of his acceptance of the Nobel Prize, Buchanan paid fulsome tribute to Wicksell's influence on his work, stating that: 'Many of my contributions, and especially those in political economy and fiscal theory, might be described as varied reiterations, elaborations, and extensions of Wicksellian themes' (LFCL, p. 455).[1]

Wicksell was, Buchanan continued, 'the most important precursor of modern public choice theory' because Wicksell had set out the three basic foundational principles of the public choice approach: *methodological individualism*; the *motivational symmetry* of political and economic actors (seen particularly vividly in the notion that the political process might be used for exploitative purposes, implying that political actors are not necessarily altruistic); and the conception of *politics as a form of exchange* in which people bargain over the distribution of costs and benefits in an attempt to agree mutually advantageous outcomes (LFCL, pp. 456–461; See also: LoL, p. 50).

There are, of course, many thinkers whose work may be identified as a precursor of public choice theory. The social contract theorists Thomas Hobbes, John Locke and Jean-Jacques Rousseau, for example, were clearly an important influence on Buchanan's work and are the subject of extensive discussion in Buchanan's principal elucidation of the political theoretic dimensions of public choice in his book *The Limits of Liberty*. But there is no doubt that Knut Wicksell was the one thinker whose work anticipated the public choice approach in most significant respects.

Buchanan left Chicago in 1948 with the award of a PhD for his thesis, *Fiscal Equity in a Federal State*, supervised by Roy Blough and Frank Knight, a study of the different possible standards and criteria central governments might use to determine the redistribution of revenue between smaller political units within a federal political system. Although Buchanan's PhD would lead to publications in important economic journals, and federalism would remain an important theme throughout his work, as will be discussed in

Chapter 2, it was probably his encounters with Frank Knight and Knut Wicksell that were the most important and most enduring legacies of Buchanan's three years at the University of Chicago.

Knoxville, Tallahassee and the Italian Year

Buchanan left Chicago to take up an appointment as an Associate Professor of Economics at the University of Tennessee at Knoxville, in part because the fellowship that had helped to fund his graduate studies required that he returned to the South on completion of his studies. At Knoxville Buchanan worked 'as a straightforward public finance economist, whose concerns were about taxes, budgets, federalism, and fiscal policy' (EFTOI, p. 83).

As described earlier, Buchanan had spent an academically unsatisfying year as a student at Knoxville prior to his conscription into the navy and similarly as a faculty member he found the intellectual environment at Knoxville uninspired and uninspiring. Although he was promoted to a full professor in 1950, two years after his initial appointment, he recalled that there 'was then . . . an academic "deadness" about the whole Knoxville institution' (EFTOI, p. 196). This was the principal reason why Buchanan accepted an offer of a position at the expanding Florida State University in Tallahassee in 1951. It was at Tallahassee, more than at the University of Chicago, that Buchanan achieved 'an awareness of the excitement of ideas' that he had not experienced before (EFTOI, p. 197). Buchanan attributed this awareness to the iconoclastic intellectual atmosphere at Tallahassee where a faculty of 'young Turks' were willing and able to challenge the conventional wisdom of the economics discipline. Whereas Chicago was the institution most closely associated with mainstream economics, at Tallahassee a group of young scholars sought to challenge the disciplinary conventions. In particular, Buchanan co-authored with colleagues Clark Allen and Marshall Colberg an elementary economics textbook that provided ample opportunity to critically explore the foundations of orthodox public finance scholarship.

It was in the intellectually stimulating environment of Tallahassee that Buchanan published two articles in the *Journal of Political Economy* that demonstrated his extraordinary scholarly potential. The first was a critique of Kenneth Arrow's (1951) hugely influential book, *Social Choice and Individual Values*. Buchanan argued that Arrow's attempt to set out the requirements of an ordering of social values that accurately reflected the preferences of individual members of society was 'inappropriate for a democratic society' given that individual values and preferences must by definition be inconsistent and incommensurable. For Buchanan, Arrow's attempt to discover the mechanisms via which consistent collective preferences may be established negated the fundamentally *individual* nature of individual preferences (LFCL, p. 16; LFCL, pp. 89–102).

The second article was a comparison of individual choice in voting and the market, setting out systematically the importance of institutional context to people's choices. Buchanan argued, for example, that because in democratic decision-making people were uncertain how their peers would vote, whereas in a market context other people's choices were of only secondary importance, individuals with the same preferences would make different choices when faced with ostensibly the same decision in voting and in the market (LFCL, pp. 75–88).

These two articles were seminal early contributions to the economics of politics, staking out the territory that would later become the domain of public choice theory.

In 1954 Buchanan successfully applied for a Fulbright scholarship to spend a year in Italy reading classic Italian works in public finance. Buchanan had already read an English translation of De Viti De Marco's *First Principles of Public Finance*, which had inspired him to learn more about an earlier generation of Italian scholars who had developed a methodological individualist approach to the analysis of public finance that also took into account the realities of collective decision-making, rejecting the assumption that government was always benevolent, and thereby avoiding many of the pitfalls of the work of more orthodox American and British scholars (EFTOI, pp. 82–84).

Buchanan and his wife spent a year in Italy from September 1955 to August 1956. Buchanan immersed himself in Italian culture and public finance scholarship and also found time to complete an English translation of Wickell's essay on just taxation.

Buchanan's Italian year had a profound impact on his life and work. On his return to America he abandoned a partially written book in orthodox public finance theory and instead began work on a new book, *Public Principles of Public Debt*, which drew upon his readings in classical Italian public finance and Wicksell to challenge the orthodox analysis of public debt. According to the orthodox view, public debt created via domestic borrowing does not make society poorer because no money leaves the domestic economy. Rather, money is transferred from one domestic source (lenders) to another (government) and then repaid with interest over time. At no point does the total sum of wealth in the economy change as a result of this process of debt creation. However, Buchanan argued that if internal public debt creation was analysed at the level of the individual, following Wicksell and the Italian public finance theorists, then it became clear that public debt was not economically neutral, akin to an individual moving money between their different bank accounts, but in fact involved the transfer of income and wealth from some people to others, creating winners and losers. The economic impact of such a process, Buchanan argued, could only be evaluated in terms of the gains and losses experienced by each individual, rather than via a calculus of gains and losses at the societal level.

Buchanan's early encounters with Wicksell and then the Italian public finance theorists enabled him to see questions of political economy in new and often unique ways. Reflecting later in his career on the influences that shaped his work, Buchanan wrote: 'Knut Wicksell and the Italians left me with an enduring intellectual legacy that insured personal differentiation of "my product" from that of most of my peers' (EFTOI, p. 91).

Virginia Political Economy

The work of Buchanan and his collaborators in the field of political economy is often referred to as Virginia public choice, or Virginia political economy, in reference to the US state where a succession of academic institutions housed a succession of institutional centres for public choice scholarship. Virginia public choice is usually contrasted with the work in public choice that developed concurrently at the University of Chicago, though the extent to which Virginia and Chicago public choice are intellectually distinct, rather than just geographically distinct, may be debated. If there is a sharp intellectual distinction between the two schools it may be that Virginia public choice theorists have focused on the constitutional metaframework of rules and conventions within which political decision-making takes place, whereas Chicago public choice scholars have tended to apply standard micro-economic and quantitative analysis to the political realm without any particular focus on the constitutional dimension. Nevertheless, there are certainly scholars strongly associated with the Virginian tradition whose work would seem to fit comfortably with the approach of most Chicago-based public choice scholars – Gordon Tullock would be a prime example. It is probable, then, that the Virginia and Chicago public choice approaches represent an intellectual continuum rather than two separate and distinct camps.

It may be appropriate, then, that, according to Buchanan, Virginia public choice 'was born in the foyer of the Social Sciences Building at the University of Chicago early in 1948'. It was here that Buchanan had a conversation with fellow Chicago graduate student G. Warren Nutter in which they discovered a shared concern with the increasing emphasis on formal technique in contemporary economics and a shared desire to find an institutional setting in which the discipline could return to its classical origins 'as a component element in a comprehensive moral philosophy' (EFTOI, p. 94).

Charlottesville

The conversation between Buchanan and Nutter in Chicago was to bear fruit nearly ten years later when the two men were reunited as professorial appointments at the University of Virginia in Charlottesville in 1956 and 1957 respectively. At Charlottesville, the university administration was 'more than passively receptive' to Buchanan's proposal to establish a political economy centre that would challenge the dominant thrust of the economics discipline at that time. In 1957 the Thomas Jefferson Center for Studies in Political Economy and Social Philosophy was established with an explicit aim to create a 'community of scholars who wish to preserve a social order based on individual liberty' (IPE, pp. 39–40).

The Thomas Jefferson Center was an extraordinary success: a number of leading scholars were appointed to the faculty including future Nobel Prize winner Ronald Coase, Gordon Tullock and Leland Yeager; a host of eminent scholars made half-year visits to the centre, including future Nobel laureates F. A. Hayek and Maurice Allais, as well as Frank Knight, Michael Polanyi, Bruno Leoni and Duncan Black; a large number of high-quality graduate students studied at the centre, many of whom would go on to successful careers in the discipline, including Craig Stubblebine, Robert Tollison and Richard Wagner.

Gordon Tullock arrived in Charlottesville in 1958 as a post-doctoral fellow. Tullock had spent close to a decade as a civil servant in the US foreign office and had written a manuscript on bureaucracy which Buchanan described as 'a fascinating analysis of modern government bureaucracy that was almost totally buried in an irritating personal narrative account of Tullock's nine-year experience in the foreign service hierarchy' (IPE, p. 98). Tullock's book remained unpublished until Buchanan edited it into a publishable state some years later, excising Tullock's personal narrative in the process. This happened, however, after Buchanan and Tullock collaborated on what is probably the most famous single work in the Virginia political economy corpus, *The Calculus of Consent.*

The Calculus of Consent was largely written during the 1959–60 academic year, when Buchanan had a sabbatical year without teaching responsibilities and Tullock had temporarily left Charlottesville for a position in the foreign affairs department at the University of South Carolina. Half a century on, the public choice approach has become so familiar and influential that it may be hard to capture how groundbreaking *The Calculus of Consent* was on first publication in 1962. The book applied the methodological individualism and assumption of self-interested motivation standard to economic analysis to the analysis of political institutions. Holding these elements constant, Buchanan and Tullock were able to systematically analyse the impact of different political arrangements, such as different voting rules, unicameralism and bicameralism, and vote-trading, on collective choice.

Buchanan and Tullock intended *The Calculus of Consent* to be a defence of the American democratic ideal of a constitutional system of checks and balances that placed clear limits on government power, as had been originally envisaged by the American Founders, particularly James Madison, the principal author of the US Constitution. Indeed, Buchanan and Tullock wrote that:

> [T]he Madisonian theory, either that which is explicitly contained in Madison's writings or that which is embodied in the American constitutional system, may be compared with the normative theory that emerges from the economic approach [in this work]. (CoC, p. 24)

Some years later, Buchanan wrote along similar lines that the intended message of the book was that: 'Democracy works, if organized along the lines of the American constitutional republic' (EFROI, p. 113).

Yet the stark warning of the inherent dangers of unconstrained democracy contained within *The Calculus of Consent* and other works by Buchanan has led many critics to view Buchanan's work (and public choice theory more generally) as normatively anti-democratic (e.g. Kelman, 1988; Petracca, 1991; Self, 1993; Shapiro, 1996). In reality, as will be set out in more detail in the next chapter, at the heart of Buchanan's work is a normative commitment to democracy, but to democracy understood as a system of government that protects individual liberty from the real and ever-present threat of politically-imposed tyranny.

The Thomas Jefferson Center at Charlottesville was extraordinarily successful in terms of the production of groundbreaking work in political economy, the attraction of leading scholars as permanent and visiting faculty, the recruitment of high quality research students, and publication of research in the most prestigious international outlets. Unfortunately, the university administration was unappreciative of the centre's success and instead became concerned with the 'political motivation' of the centre, particularly in the context of what seemed to be the social and political mood of the day.

In 1960 America had elected John F. Kennedy as president, a man who, in his inauguration address, had told the nation to 'Ask not what your country can do for you – ask what you can do for your country', setting out a vision of the relationship between the US government and its citizens that seemed at odds with the limited constitutional republic envisaged by the Founders and held to be an ideal model by Buchanan and his colleagues. As Buchanan later recalled, the research agenda of the public choice scholars at the University of Virginia that was inherently sceptical of government but set firmly within the Madisonian tradition, seemed markedly out of step with the times:

> We were not allowed, at least in Charlottesville, Virginia, to pursue the grand endeavour that was Madison's, even in our abstract research inquiry. We were chastised, scorned, and differentially damaged by our stated refusals to ride with the gathering winds of Camelot. How could we, as rational human beings, fail to sense the

glory of the hour? Our external academic successes, both in training graduate students and in professional publications of our research, were as nothing when matched against our alleged "fascist" and "right-wing" zealotry by those who made decisions for the corporate actor that was the University of Virginia. (EFTOI, p. 113)

In 1963 the university administration commissioned a secret committee to investigate the activities of the Thomas Jefferson Center. This committee produced a report without any contact with or input from the center that concluded that the economics faculty at the university was 'rigidly committed to a single point of view' which it labelled as 'nineteenth-century ultra-conservatism' (IPE, p. 43).

The university administration sought to change what it saw as the unacceptable ideological character of its economics faculty by appointing economists who were deemed 'modern' in outlook and by ceasing to actively retain existing members of the faculty. This strategy was successful, so that within five years the economics faculty at Charlottesville was no longer distinct from that of any other mainstream American university. In 1967 Gordon Tullock left to become Professor of Economics and Political Science at Rice University. A year later Buchanan left to take up an appointment at UCLA and in 1969 Warren Nutter exited to join President Nixon's staff. It seemed that the notion of a distinct Virginia public choice was over.

UCLA and 'academia in anarchy'

At the University of California at Los Angeles Buchanan joined an 'excellent, and highly professional', economics department. But he was quickly to judge the move to Los Angeles 'a personal mistake' because of the tumult on campus that was being created by large-scale student protests (EFTOI, p. 114). At UCLA Buchanan found himself at one of the principal centres of the protests against US military involvement in Vietnam and the perceived discrimination against African Americans within the institutions of the US government.

In his published writings Buchanan has never made a formal pronouncement on the rightness or wrongness of the Vietnam War, although he has cited US military involvement in Vietnam as an example of the exercise of excessive executive power, suggesting that the constitutional basis of the war may be questioned (LoL, p. 217–218). Buchanan has, however, described protests in support of the rights of African American citizens as being 'motivated by wholly admirable precepts for achieving racial justice' (LoL, p. 218). Nevertheless, Buchanan 'came down squarely on the "law and order" side of most of the critical issues that surfaced' and 'could not understand at all the behavior of my peers in the nation's academies' who gave explicit or tacit support to the student protestors (EFTIO, p. 114).

Buchanan felt that the student protests exploited the fact that universities were organized according to unwritten rules that were voluntarily observed by members of the university community without the need for formal enforcement. The voluntary and informal nature of these conventions made universities particularly vulnerable to protests aimed at the disruption of university life:

> Protest came to be the order of the day in the late years of the decade [the 1960s]. Venerable institutions that had long survived by adherence to unwritten behavioral rules, workable ordered anarchies such as universities, proved to be exceedingly vulnerable to disruption

once voluntary respect for the rules broke down. (LoL, p. 218)

For Buchanan, the appropriate response to such disruption was formal and strict enforcement of the rules. Failure to do so was to jeopardize the rule of law by turning the decision-making processes over to the minority engaged in protest and thereby incentivizing further and more disruptive protests. In Buchanan's view, the university administration at UCLA failed to respond in such an appropriate and effective manner to the student protests (LoL, p. 218; EFTOI, p. 114; AiA, Chapter 8).

These events had a profound effect on Buchanan. *The Calculus of Consent* had been written as a defence of the American system of government, but, for Buchanan, the events of the late 1960s seemed to show the fundamental and profound failure of that system. First, the government had adopted many policies that were incompatible with the notion of limited, constitutional government founded upon popular consent. Second, the government had then failed in its most basic duty to preserve the rule of law in its response to protests against these unpopular policies. The events of the 1960s seemed to show that the US system of constitutional checks and balances was in fact unable to preserve the basic legal framework necessary for a free society founded upon individual liberty (LoL, pp. 216–219).

Furthermore, those institutions of civil society that had operated according to an 'ordered anarchy' of mutual cooperation and reciprocation appeared to have been seriously undermined by the social upheaval of the decade. Buchanan cited the changes that had taken place in American universities as one example of this process. With Nicos Devletoglou, a political economist at the London School of Economics who had held a visiting position at UCLA during Buchanan's tenure there, Buchanan co-authored an analysis of the crisis he saw engulfing American universities titled *Academia in Anarchy*. Buchanan has since distanced himself from this work (e.g. EFTOI, p. 115), and it was not included in his Collected Works published by Liberty Fund, but it nevertheless serves as a useful historical statement of Buchanan's fears for the fate of American universities and American society in the face of unprecedented unrest and upheaval (AiA, particularly Chapter 8).

At UCLA Buchanan 'sensed an urge to stand and fight, to do battle in the quads', in defence of the 'rules and conventions' that were being destroyed by 'the new barbarians' (EFTOI, p. 115). But Buchanan also knew that such a rearguard action was unlikely to prove successful and was almost certainly not where his personal comparative advantage lay. He decided instead to retreat to 'the netherlands of academia' where he could continue his work unmolested. An opportunity arose to return to Virginia where in 1968 Gordon Tullock had re-established the public choice centre as the Center for Study of Public Choice at Virginia Polytechnic Institute in Blacksburg. In 1969 Buchanan departed from UCLA to rejoin his former colleagues in Blacksburg.

Blacksburg

As a technical institute with only a small, unremarkable economics department, Virginia Polytechnic Institute might have seemed an unpromising home for the Center for Study of Public Choice. In fact, the clear separation of the economics department and the Public Choice Center removed the pressure, or perhaps the temptation, for those working at the Center to engage in mainstream economic tuition alongside their research activities. Whereas at Charlottesville time and intellectual energy had been diverted to teaching about the market process, at Blacksburg scholarly activities were focused exclusively on research into political processes (IPE, p. 58).

Another fortuitous aspect of the location at Virginia Tech was the housing of the Center in the Old President's House, a large colonial mansion set in woods secluded from the rest of the campus. The internal architecture of the House, with offices around the sides of each floor and a large central space that served as a hub and meeting room, enabled scholars to close their doors if engaged in work requiring intense concentration and open their doors to visitors, or converse in the central space, at other times. In the words of Geoffrey Brennan, one of Buchanan's most important collaborators, the building 'turned out to be a wonderfully constructed space for the kind of academic enterprise that the Center was' (Brennan, 2004, p. 90).

These architectural and intellectual advantages were built upon by the organizational culture that developed through the leadership and example of senior scholars like Buchanan and Tullock. In most universities the majority of academic staff do their research work from home, only coming into the university to teach or perform administrative tasks, so that many academic departments are full of empty offices most days. Buchanan's working practice was to be at his university office desk from 6 a.m. to 6 p.m., six days a week plus a half day on Sunday, and he instilled an expectation of presenteeism among the scholars at the Public Choice Center. Whereas many academics may only rarely have a meaningful intellectual discussion with colleagues, at the Virginia Tech Center such interactions took place on a daily basis (Brennan, 2004; McKenzie, 2004).

At Blacksburg Buchanan's intellectual focus shifted in response to the turbulent social situation in America that had been powerfully brought home to him during his year at UCLA. Whereas at Charlottesville Buchanan's work had focused on the ways that democratic processes might mediate diverse preferences to produce collective outcomes, now his attention turned to the problem of anarchy and the inherently fragile nature of social and political order (IPE, p. 58).

For Buchanan, the most pressing research problem 'seemed to be to explain and understand the emergence of order out of anarchy rather than to grasp the meaning of a stable order that had already existed' (IPE, p. 58). It was at this time that Winston C. Bush, a young scholar who shared Buchanan's interest in the possibility of social order emerging out of anarchy, joined the Public Choice Center. In the words of Buchanan, Bush was 'the catalyst who helped us put it all together' (IPE, p. 58). Bush organized a series of weekly workshops at the Center in which participants presented papers on the subject of anarchy. Gordon Tullock later collected the papers in two small volumes published by the Blacksburg centre and titled *Explorations in the Theory of Anarchy* (1972) and *Further Explorations in the Theory of Anarchy* (1974).

Bush was tragically killed in a car accident at the age of 33 in 1973, but in his lifetime he did publish the seminal contribution to the volume *Explorations in the Theory of Anarchy*. In his chapter, 'Individual Welfare in Anarchy', Bush developed a formal economic model to show that in anarchy, or the state of nature, rules to define private property rights should emerge because it is to each individual's mutual advantage not to expend unnecessary effort defending their property from the threat of predation.

However, the property rights that emerge from anarchy are unlikely to protect the original distribution of resources, but rather represent an accommodation among the interests of the different individuals. In other words, in order to secure a peaceful settlement in which property rights are respected by all it may be necessary to assign a greater share of income and wealth to particularly ruthless individuals than might otherwise be considered just or fair (Bush, 1972).[2]

The death of Winston Bush was a substantial blow to the Public Choice Center. Buchanan later reflected that, 'After Bush's tragic death in 1973, it was difficult to recapture the Blacksburg spirit that had been so alive during the winter in which we studied anarchy' (EFTOI, p. 102). But the studies in anarchy that Bush organized and Bush's seminal paper on the subject were significant influences on what is probably Buchanan's single most important work, his book *The Limits of Liberty: Between Anarchy and Leviathan* that was published in 1975 with a dedication to the memory of Bush (LoL, p. 32; EFTOI, p. 12).

The Limits of Liberty is a book that ranges across economics, social philosophy and political philosophy to explore the basis of social order and, in particular, whether a state can emerge out of anarchy with universal consent and whether such a state can then be controlled so it does not threaten the peace it was created to maintain. In common with Bush's analysis and the argument of Gordon Tullock's *The Social Dilemma* (1974) which also emerged from the Blacksburg seminars on anarchy, Buchanan concluded that anarchy was inherently unstable: rational self-interested individuals would choose to enter into a social contract to create the state for mutual protection and advantage rather than remain in the state of nature where the threat of violent predation was ever present and many collective action problems would be impossible to overcome.

The Public Choice Center at Blacksburg remained the centre of the public choice universe with a unique scholarly culture until the early 1980s when tensions between the Virginia Tech administration and the Center began to emerge. These tensions were not akin to the ideological conflicts that had become manifest at Charlottesville, but rather, according to Buchanan's account, resulted from the decision by the university administration to build the institution's strength in mainstream economics as a counterpoint to the public choice program. As part of this process, the shaping of the future of the economics program at Blacksburg was transferred from the Public Choice Center under Buchanan's leadership to the economics department. As news of the discontent created by this change spread beyond Blacksburg, a number of other universities approached the Center with a view to exploring the possibility of a move to a new institutional location (EFTOI, pp. 188–190).

Fairfax

George Mason University in Fairfax, Virginia, was established as a branch of the University of Virginia in 1957 and became an independent institution in 1972. In its relatively short existence it has been become a world-leading academic centre in many fields, including economics. It was entrepreneurs at George Mason University, notably the Austrian economist and then chair of the economics department Karen I. Vaughn who successfully negotiated the move of the Public Choice Center from Blacksburg to their university in 1982.

At George Mason University the Virginia public choice tradition continues in what Buchanan certainly believes to be its natural home:

> [Virginia political economy] I have found to be appropriately described locationally in the commonwealth that produced James Madison and the other Virginia Founders. I can, I think, make a plausible case that this framework would be out of place in California, Illinois, or Massachusetts. (EFTOI, p. 106)

For Buchanan, then, Virginia public choice is inextricably bound up with the American Founders' desire to create a constitutional settlement that captured the benefits of collective organization and protected the liberty of individuals from the threat of predation and exploitation whether in the state of nature or via the state itself. Virginia, as the US state most closely linked to the American Founders, would seem to be the natural place to locate such an intellectual enterprise.

Nobel Prize and Beyond

Buchanan was about to leave his house for work at George Mason University at 6.32 a.m. on 16 October 1986 when he received the call from Stockholm informing him that he had been awarded the Nobel Prize. The award of the Nobel Prize proved to be a life-changing event, transforming Buchanan from a relatively little-known academic in a relatively little-known university into an international celebrity, in great demand for lectures, talks and seminars at academic and quasi-academic institutions across the world (EFTOI, Chapter 11).

Buchanan's receipt of the Nobel Prize was the starting point of this chapter and in many ways it is also an appropriate place to end. But this is not to suggest that the Nobel Prize in any way marked the end of Buchanan's career or intellectual contribution. Although a Nobel Prize may often be the crowning recognition of a lifetime's work, after 1986 Buchanan continued his formidable output of books and articles, so that by the time of the publication of the twentieth volume of his Collected Works by Liberty Fund in 2002, Buchanan's curriculum vitae took up 45 pages of that volume and listed 28 books and literally hundreds of journal articles. Although Buchanan celebrated his eightieth birthday in 1999 and his ninetieth in 2009, further books and articles continued to be produced with no discernable reduction in quality. This phenomenal productivity across many decades is testament to the value of Buchanan's work ethic summed up on his often repeated adage that academic success first and foremost involves people 'applying their backside to the backside of their chairs' (e.g. McKenzie, 2004, p. 22).

James M. Buchanan died on 9 January 2013. His life and career are an example of how much can be achieved by a combination of ability and effort. Of course, Buchanan was undoubtedly an exceptional individual in both regards, but his life is nevertheless a demonstration of what could be achieved by an individual from relatively humble origins in twentieth-century America. In the context of the present book, however, the significance of Buchanan's life lies less in his personal achievement and more in his contribution to knowledge – and to conservative and libertarian thought in particular. The next chapter will present Buchanan's key ideas as they relate to social, economic and political thought.

Notes

1. Johnson (2006) has challenged the widely held belief that Buchanan's interpretation of Wicksell is correct and that therefore Buchanan can be properly described as Wicksell's heir. Even if Johnson is correct that Buchanan and others have misinterpreted important aspects of Wicksell's thesis, it nevertheless remains the case that Wicksell's writing on public finance was an important influence on Buchanan's approach and thus on public choice theory more generally.
2. For a contemporary discussion of Bush's article and related issues, as well the reproduction of the original essays contained in both *Explorations in the Theory of Anarchy* and *Further Explorations in the Theory of Anarchy*, see the collection edited by Stringham (2005).

Chapter 2

Buchanan's Ideas

Introduction

I remain, in basic values, an individualist, a constitutionalist, a contractarian, a democrat – terms that mean essentially the same thing to me.

(*LoL, p. 11*)

James Buchanan has been a remarkably consistent thinker. In the words of Romer (1988, p. 167), his work 'has displayed a remarkable consistency of theme and outlook over his career'. From his early papers published in the 1950s, through his major publications spanning the final four decades of the twentieth century, to his most recent works in the twenty-first century, Buchanan has not deviated from his essential individualist, constitutionalist, contractarian, democratic vision.

Although Buchanan's ideas developed and advanced through more than fifty years of scholarship – in particular he became much more sceptical of the efficacy of contemporary democratic institutions from the late 1960s onwards – much of Buchanan's intellectual output has involved multiple reiterations and applications of the same basic principles. Indeed, one of Buchanan's guiding principles, following the counsel of his teacher Frank Knight, was that ideas and arguments require continual reiteration if they are to be accepted by sceptical minds (e.g. RoR, p. 130).

This chapter sets out the core of Buchanan's intellectual contribution to social, economic and political thought. It does not deal with Buchanan's contributions to technical economics, such as his work on the theory of externalities and clubs; although these are important contributions in their own right they are not essential to, and indeed may detract from, the presentation of Buchanan's core contribution that is the task of this chapter.

After this introductory section, the second part of this chapter will present the starting point of Buchanan's thought in 'the individualist postulate': the belief that only individuals can purposefully pursue ends and that therefore 'society' should be understood as in essence an amalgam of the individuals who compose it. All of Buchanan's ideas follow from this basic methodological individualist premise. The third part of the chapter will begin the presentation of Buchanan's account of the possibilities and pathologies of democratic politics with consideration of Buchanan's explanation of why people leave the state of nature to enter into political arrangements. Here, Buchanan argues that people contract into the state because they consider this the least-worst option in comparison to the problems they encounter in anarchy. The fourth section will consider the role of rights in Buchanan's theory of the shift from the state of nature into the social contract and, in particular, Buchanan's rejection of the doctrine of natural rights. The fifth section will consider 'the constitutional moment': the process by which individuals enter into political agreement. In particular, this section will set out the role of unanimity in Buchanan's model of constitutional agreement. The sixth part of the chapter will consider the supply of public goods by the state and the agreement of non-unanimous decision-making rules for post-constitutional choices. The seventh part will emphasize Buchanan's normative commitment to democracy that is the core of his philosophical outlook and consider its implications for the argument herein. The eighth and longest part of the chapter will consider the problems that people face in the political realm after the social contract has been agreed. Here, Buchanan identified four crucial (and linked) problems of politics: the disparity that may exist between individual preferences and the collective decisions made via the political process; the problem that the political process may be used by some to exploit or impose external costs on others; the problem of political rent-seeking; and the problem of the creation of a state that is invested with a monopoly on the legitimate use of force within a given society. The ninth section will present Buchanan's solutions to the problems of politics that all involve the application of the principle of constitutionalism. A short final section will conclude.

The Individualist Postulate

The key foundational assumption of Buchanan's thought is methodological individualism. In the opening section of his single most important philosophical contribution, *The Limits of Liberty,* Buchanan stated: 'My approach is profoundly *individualistic,* in an ontological-methodological sense' (LoL, p. 3). Similarly, in the opening chapter of *The Calculus of Consent,* Buchanan and Tullock wrote:

Our theory thus begins with the acting or decision-making individual as he participates in the processes through which group choices are organized. Since our model incorporates individual behavior as its central feature, our "theory" can perhaps best be classified as being *methodologically* individualistic. (CoC, p. 3)

Methodological individualism can be understood as a way of viewing the world and also as a social science research strategy. As a way of viewing the world, methodological individualism implies that there is no such thing as 'society' other than the sum of the individuals who compose it. It is only individuals who can act, choose or hold beliefs. In the words of Buchanan:

Only individuals choose; only individuals act. An understanding of any social interaction process must be based on an analysis of the choice behavior of persons who participate in the process. Results that are predicted or that may be observed in social interaction must be factored down into the separate choices made by individuals. (MSMO, p. 56)

The actions of societies, governments or firms, then, can only be understood in terms of individual agency. It is an error to speak of the 'public interest', or to say that 'society' believes something, when empirically only individuals can pursue interests or hold beliefs. It is held, then, that there are no transcendental 'social' or 'public' values or ends, only the values and ends that different individuals happen to have.

As a research agenda, methodological individualism implies that social phenomena, whether the prices that exist in economic markets, the modern institutions of government or the folk beliefs of isolated primordial tribes, should be studied in terms of the choices, beliefs and values of the individuals who populate those markets, institutions or tribes.

All of Buchanan's work follows from his conviction that it is only possible to understand society in terms of the individuals who compose it; any other approach to understanding the world is empirically flawed. Indeed, Buchanan has been scathing in his assessment of the value of the work of scholars who do not utilize a methodological individualist approach:

> Those who prefer to conduct inquiry into the relationships among classes, states, and other organizations as such, and without attempts to reduce analysis to the individuals who participate, do not, in my view, pass muster as social scientists in any useful sense of the term. (MSMO, p. 67)

Buchanan's work, then, is founded on the belief that there is no such thing as the 'public interest', the 'general welfare' or the 'common good': '"Social welfare" cannot be defined independently, since, as such, it cannot exist' (RoR, p. 27; See also: CoC, Chapter 2; LoL, Chapter 6). This means that when political actors do seek to pursue the 'public interest' they must, in reality, pursue their own subjective perceptions of what actions they believe to be in the public interest – in other words they must pursue their own interests because empirically they cannot know with certainty what actions are consistent with the 'public interest' (LoL, Chapter 6).

None of this implies, however, that individuals are perceived to be akin to atoms that exist in isolation from one another, untouched by other people and the external world.

On the contrary, Buchanan has argued that individuals must be located 'in four-dimensional space-time': people must be understood to live in particular places and at particular times and hence must be located in their social context. Hence, individual values will be formed in the context of people's interactions with one another within a particular institutional framework. Nevertheless, the crucial ontological fact remains that, 'Each person, as a separately existent unit of consciousness, looks at, hears, feels, and tastes that which is confronted through a "different window"' (PFPC, p. 11).

Buchanan's methodological individualism informs an ethical individualist position based upon the Kantian moral precept that individuals must always be treated as ends and never as means. No individual has any more or less moral worth than any other person and therefore no individual may be sacrificed for the benefit of other individuals or 'society'. For Buchanan, this Kantian premise is the foundation of democracy: 'democratic values must be founded on the basic Kantian notion that individual human beings are the ultimate ethical units, that persons are to be treated strictly as ends and never as means, and that there are no transcendental, suprapersonal norms' (DT, p. 37).

It follows, then, that even if we consider the choices that other people make to be in some way erroneous, public policy should not used as a means to impose our preferences upon them:

> Individual freedom becomes the overriding objective for social policy, not as an instrumental element in attaining economic or cultural bliss, and not as some metaphysically superior value, but much more simply as a necessary consequence of an individualist-democratic

methodology. In some personal and private baring of my soul, I may not 'like' the observed results of a regime that allows other men to be free . . . but the point to be emphasized is that the dominant role of individual liberty is imposed by an acceptance of the methodology of individualism and not by the subjective valuations of this or that social philosopher. (LoL, pp. 5–6)

For Buchanan, a commitment to democracy implies allowing other people to make choices that we may dislike, because if we believe in the inherent equal moral worth of each individual then each individual must be free to make their own choices.

The individualist basis of democracy is said to mean that an 'idealized politics must remain substantively empty of specific content' (PPNI, p. 20). Politics should be understood *ideally* as a mechanism via which people pursue their own individual ends, not as a forum through which the true 'public interest' or 'common good' is selected, discovered or pursued. If politics becomes a forum for collective truth-seeking, then, in the words of Buchanan and Congleton, 'ordinary persons are no longer the ultimate sovereigns but are, instead, subject to the value standards dictated by those individuals or institutions that claim access to fonts of revealed or discovered truth' (PPNI, p. 24; See also: LoL, Chapter 1).

The belief that there is no objective 'public interest' means that no substantive outcome of social organization or public policy can be judged preferable to any other, except in so far as a particular outcome may enable individuals to attain their own ends:

Each man counts for one, and that is that . . . A criterion for 'betterness' is suggested. A situation is judged 'good' to the extent that it allows individuals to get what they want to get, whatsoever this might be, limited only by the principle of mutual agreement. (LoL, p. 4)

To judge one particular substantive outcome as being preferable to any other is to hubristically place one's own values above the values of other people, something that infringes the basic Kantian principle that each individual must be treated as an end not a means. Indeed, the fact that there are no values external to individual men and women means that any attempt to discover or purse the 'public interest' or the 'common good' must necessarily lead to the imposition of some people's values on others in the name of the 'common good'.

The notion that there is no source of values external to individual men and women and that therefore there are no ends other than those envisaged by different individuals does not imply a society in which selfish individualists ruthlessly pursue their own hedonistic desires. Rather, the ends that individuals conceive may be altruistic, selfish or some combination of the two. As Buchanan and Tullock wrote: 'The analysis does not depend . . . upon any narrowly hedonistic or self-interest motivation of individuals in their behavior in social-choice processes. The representative individual in our models may be egoist or altruist or any combination thereof' (CoC, p. 3). Indeed, Brennan and Buchanan argued that, 'Any theory that depends for its predictions on the hypothesis that all persons behave' selfishly with single-minded devotion to the maximization of the present value of personal wealth 'at all times and in all circumstances must, of course, be rejected out of hand from ordinary introspection' (PT, p. 19).

Individuals are assumed to be self-interested only in the sense that they pursue ends that they themselves conceive;

nothing is implied about the substantive content of those ends. An individual may derive utility from the elimination of poverty, the protection of wildlife or the purchase of clothes from Prada. The pursuit of each could fall within an individual's self-interest.

The assumption of individual rationality inherent to the methodological individualist approach utilized by Buchanan similarly does not imply that people behave in predictable ways that might be considered 'rational'. In Buchanan's work, as in classical and neoclassical economics more generally, the assumption of individual rationality simply implies that individuals conceive of their own ends and then act in accordance with those ends. Hence, a rational individual is one whose preferences are transitive, so that if an individual prefers A to B and prefers B to C, he or she will also prefer A to C. An irrational or non-rational individual is one whose preferences are intransitive. This individual prefers A to B and prefers B to C, but he or she also prefers C to A. This final preference may be defined as irrational; it is impossible for this individual to rationally choose in accordance with such intransitive preferences.

The assumption that people behave rationally, then, simply means that people act in accordance with their self-conceived ends. It says nothing about what those ends might be or how 'rational' a person's actions may appear to external observers. Hence, if the members of a primordial tribe believe that sacrificing animals will please the gods and make the forests plentiful, it is perfectly rational for them to do so, however 'irrational' such behaviour may appear to people outside the tribe. Likewise, if a person with little apparent musical talent believes that they will one day become a successful musician, it is perfectly rational for them to forgo other opportunities in pursuit of this end, however 'irrational' such behaviour may appear to others (CoC, Chapter 4; MSMO, pp. 55–70).

Buchanan's methodological individualism implies that public policies must be analysed in terms of their impact on individual men and women, rather than their impact upon some notional entity termed 'society'. The practical implications of this were set out in Buchanan's early book-length critique of the post-war orthodoxy in public debt theory, *Public Principles of Public Debt*.

As noted in Chapter 1, according to the orthodox theory of public debt, public debt created by internal borrowing (that is, government borrowing from domestic rather than foreign lenders), should be viewed as a transfer of money within a society, in the same way that individuals may transfer money between their own bank accounts. Accordingly, public debt created via internal borrowing is not deemed to be welfare-reducing because society does not necessarily become poorer if money is transferred between its members. Buchanan argued, however, that a very different picture emerges when internal public debt creation is analysed at the level of the individual. Here, government borrowing from domestic lenders can be seen to involve the imposition of liabilities on some individuals (taxpayers) and the creation of wealth and guaranteed future income for others (beneficiaries of government spending and lenders, respectively). To determine whether or not public borrowing is welfare-reducing therefore requires analysis of the distribution of these benefits and burdens among different individuals. As Buchanan wrote: 'Individuals and families are the entities whose balance sheets must be examined if the effects of social decisions are to be determined' (PPPD, p. 33).

From a methodological individualist perspective, the creation of public debt via internal borrowing should not be judged to be economically neutral. Rather, it imposes burdens on some individuals, while others gain. The judgement as to whether those benefits and burdens should be accepted can only be made by the individuals concerned. For politicians, bureaucrats or academics to claim that no loss occurs from public debt creation negates the plight of those taxpayers whose income or wealth *will* fall as a result of such policies and would therefore seem to imply that their preferences, values and ends are irrelevant. The true implications of public policy, then, may be revealed only when analysis is undertaken at the level of the individual.

The Problems of Anarchy

In the quote at the head of this chapter Buchanan described himself as 'an individualist, a constitutionalist, a contractarian, [and] a democrat'. The section above set out Buchanan's individualism and the particular conception of democratic politics and policy that followed. This section now turns to Buchanan's contractarianism.

Buchanan's work falls within the social contract tradition of political thought that was propounded by early-modern thinkers like Hobbes, Locke and Rousseau and then re-established as a central strand in contemporary political philosophy by the 'new contractarians' of the second half of the twentieth century: John Rawls, Robert Nozick and Buchanan (Gordon, 1976).

The contractarian approach is a way of providing legitimacy to social and political arrangements by *imagining* that they were formed on the basis of an explicit contract voluntarily entered into by all parties, even though it is clear that such arrangements did not in practice arise as a result of any such contract. As Buchanan has written, 'factually and historically, the "social contract" is mythological . . . Individuals did not come together in some original position and mutually agree on the rules of social intercourse'. Moreover, even if at some point in history a social contract was agreed, such an agreement 'could hardly be considered to be contractually binding on all of us who have come behind' (CCC, p. 89).

Rather than providing an empirically accurate description of reality, the social contract is a device that facilitates the evaluation of real world institutions. The contractarian approach requires us to imagine whether people would voluntarily enter into the political arrangements that presently exist. According to Brennan and Buchanan, 'If the leap out of anarchy into order is indeed to be preferred by the citizenry, it must be possible to examine the establishment of government *as if* it emerges from the voluntary consent of those who are to be subject to it' (PT, p. 7). Hence, if we can imagine that people would voluntarily enter into a particular set of institutional arrangements, even if they did not empirically do so, then we can say that those arrangements have some claim to legitimacy: 'the contractarian construction itself is used retrospectively in a metaphorically legitimizing rather than historical sense' (RoR, p. 23).

Any (notional) social contract involves some diminution of freedom on the part of those who enter into it. Individuals agree to abide by a set of laws or rules and to suffer the agreed punishments if they fail to do so, or to contribute to the supply of public goods via compulsory taxation. Therefore the principal question that a social contract theory must answer is: why would people voluntarily limit their freedom in this way? In other words, why is the state of nature or anarchy considered inferior to government?

Buchanan's answer to this question begins from his cautiously pessimistic view of human nature. Although Buchanan has written that he is agnostic about human nature (LoL, p. 82), his work nevertheless involves a recognition of the 'frailty in human nature' that leads to 'the presumption that individuals could not attain the behavioral standards required for . . . anarchy to function acceptably' (CCC, p. 15; See also LoL, p. 12). Hence, Brennan and Buchanan have written: 'If people were saints or angels, the dilemmas we face would never have emerged in the first place' (RoR, p. 149). Buchanan's work follows Hume's dictum that in designing political institutions we should suppose every man to be a knave with no end other than his own private interests, even though we know that in reality people do not always behave knavishly (RoR, p. 68; Hume, 1777, p. 44).

The frailty inherent to human nature is compounded by the fact that, as described above, there is no objective 'public interest' that can be determined and pursued, only subjectively defined individual interests: 'separate individuals are separate individuals and, as such, are likely to have different aims and purposes' (CoC, p. 3). If individuals have a capacity to treat one another badly, then conflicts that arise between their different aims and purposes are unlikely to be always resolved peaceably in the state of nature. Consequently, Buchanan argues that in the 'genuinely anarchistic world . . . conflict rather than universalized cooperation is its central feature' (LoL, p. 12). Buchanan, then, accepts Hobbes's famous contention that in the absence of government the state of nature will be 'a war of each against each', so that consequently life will be 'nasty, brutish and short' (Hobbes, 1651, Chapter 13; LoL, in particular Chapter 4; RoR, in particular Chapter 4).

For a social contract to bestow legitimacy on government it has to be agreed by all parties. It will be in the interests of the great majority of people to enter into a social contract to create a state to act as a protective agency to prevent predation by the strong and powerful. But the question remains why should the strong and powerful enter into a social contract if in the state of nature they are able to gain via predatory acts against the relatively weak and powerless?

According to Buchanan (LoL, Chapter 4), the strong and powerful enter into the social contract only when/if they will gain more from so doing than they will gain from remaining in the state of nature. This may happen, in particular, because resources devoted to predation and protection in the state of nature may be reassigned to productive activities after the social contract so that even the strong and powerful gain overall from the establishment of social order by the state. In other words, there may be gains for all resulting from multilateral disarmament (LoL, pp. 76–77).

Buchanan (LoL, p. 84) has represented this situation in a formal model of a two-person Prisoner's Dilemma shown below in Figure 2.1. In this model, two people of unequal strength, A and B, each face two possible behavioural choices: to respect or not respect the rights of the other. These two behavioural choices produce four possible out-

		B	
		Respects Rights 0	Respects No Rights V
A	Respects Rights 0	Cell I 19, 7	Cell II 3, 11
	Respects No Rights V	Cell III 22, 1	Cell IV 9, 2

FIGURE 2.1

comes. The four cells of the model each show the different pay-offs that A and B receive in each of the possible outcomes. In Cell I, both A and B choose to respect the rights of the other and here A, the stronger of the two, receives a pay-off of 19 and B, the weaker, receives a pay-off of 7. However, if B chooses not to respect A's rights by taking from him or her via predation, while A continues to respect B's rights, then B receives an increased pay-off of 11, while A's pay-off is reduced to 3. If, on the other hand, A chooses not to respect B's rights by taking from him or her via predation, while B continues to respect A's rights, then A receives a much greater pay-off of 22, while B's pay-off is reduced to 1. If both decide not the respect the other's rights, then Cell IV shows the pay-offs to be 9 for A and 2 for B. Cell IV might be described as the 'natural equilibrium': the arrangement of benefits and burdens that would occur in anarchy in the absence of government.

It should be clear that the outcomes in Cells II and III are inherently unstable: it would be irrational for either person to respect the other's rights if that respect was not reciprocated, because Cell IV, where neither respects the other's rights, offers a better pay-off for the loser in Cells II or III. The real choice that the two parties face, then, is between Cells I and IV, because any movement into Cells II and III automatically leads to Cell IV. Cell I, then, represents the social contract and Cell IV represents the state of nature. The model shows that for strong A and for weak B, the social contract is preferable to the state of nature. Hence, the strong and the weak will both gain by agreeing to enter into the social contract.

In the words of Buchanan and Tullock, people agree to enter into the social contract, even though it involves constraints on their own behaviour, because 'each individual must recognize that, were he to be free to violate convention, others must be similarly free; and, as compared to this chaotic state of affairs, he will rationally choose to accept restrictions on his own behavior' (CoC, p. 315).

Importantly, the formal model presented in Figure 2.1 also shows that people do not have to be equal in terms of resources, status or power in order to voluntarily enter into a social contract. On the contrary, according to Buchanan (LoL, p. 71), 'even among men who are unequal, a structure of legal rights can be predicted to emerge, a structure that retains characteristic elements that we associate with the precepts of individualism'. That is, even people who are materially unequal will voluntarily choose to enter into a social contract that does not alter the basic facts of their inequality post-agreement, but, on the contrary recognizes and protects their basic rights, including their 'right' to unequal holdings that may be the result of violent predation prior to the social contract.[1]

Rights

The account of the problems of anarchy that lead people to voluntarily enter into the social contract presented in the section above necessitates some consideration of the role of rights in Buchanan's explanation of the passage from the state of nature to political agreement.

Perhaps surprisingly, Buchanan rejects (what we might call) a Lockean natural rights approach that forms the basis of much classical liberal and libertarian philosophy. According to this approach, people are assumed to possess natural rights (that is, inalienable, basic rights irrespective of the existence of any political authority willing to recognize and protect those rights) and the creation of the state principally involves recognition of these pre-existing rights (See Mack, 2009, particularly Chapters 2, 3 and 4).

Buchanan rejects the notion that people have natural rights because their existence would imply a source of values external to individual men and women. As Brennan and Buchanan have written: 'The contractarian derives all value from individual participants in the community and rejects externally defined sources of value, including "natural rights"' (RoR, p. 25; See also CoC, pp. 314–315).

It is argued that rights cannot exist independently of the values of individual men and women; rights are created when people choose to respect the persons and properties of others. In the state of nature, or anarchy, widespread agreement to respect the rights of others has not yet been reached and so rights cannot be said to exist. Such an agreement is part of the process via which people leave the state of nature and enter into the social contract. Rights can only be said to exist when there is general agreement to respect the rights of others and this agreement has been formalized into law (EPET, p. 4).

In this respect Buchanan's work is much closer to Rawls than to Nozick. Rawls (1971, pp. 94–96) similarly located rights in the agreement of the social contract, so that rights follow from practical reasoning in which individuals determine their values and the set of rights that should properly accompany those values. Nozick (1974, p. ix), on the other hand, famously began his classic of political philosophy, *Anarchy, State, and Utopia*, with the assertion that 'Individuals have rights', a claim that individuals have natural rights that exist prior to formal political agreement between persons.

Political Agreement and Constitutional Choice: Enter the State

For Buchanan, anarchy is an undesirable condition in which all individuals are subject to predation, or the threat of predation, and are therefore compelled to devote significant resources to protection. This creates a 'race to the bottom' in which evermore resources are allocated to protection and evermore people engage in plunder until society descends into a chaotic Hobbesian war of all against all. Even for the strong and powerful, the costs of predation and protection become so high that anarchy will be considered inferior to life under a political authority. In order to escape from this undesirable state of affairs, people agree to constrain their own and other people's behaviour by entering into a social contract.

In entering into a social contract, people are faced with the crucial question of what constitutional rules and institutional arrangements are to be selected. These 'rules of the game' will determine the rights of individuals, and the likely distribution of benefits and burdens, and obligations and entitlements, into the future. Constitutional choice, then, concerns *choice of rules* rather than *choice within rules* (CoC, p. 4; LoL, Chapter 4; RoR, Chapter 1).

Buchanan and other scholars working within the framework of constitutional political economy approach this choice of rules as a process of exchange analogous to economic transactions in private markets.

In the economic marketplace, individuals exchange goods and services that they value (or the ability to purchase goods and services) for other goods and services that they value more highly (or the ability to purchase those more-valued goods and services). Market exchanges, therefore, only take place when an exchange is mutually advantageous. Similarly, in entering into political agreement, individuals exchange some of their freedom (which we may imagine they value) for the benefits of social order enforced by political authority (which we must assume they value more highly).

A social contract, it is argued, it is not imposed from the top-down by an almighty sovereign power, nor does it result from the actions of one powerful group within society. Rather, a social contract should be modelled as the result of multilateral agreement among individuals. Hence, according to the contractarian approach, 'the whole enterprise of politics can be viewed only as a complex many-person system of exchanges or contracts' (RoR, p. 30; See also: CoC, Chapter 3; LoL, Chapter 4).

Market exchanges will only take place with the agreement of all exchanging parties. In this sense, market exchanges require the unanimous consent of participants and only take place when the exchanges supply Pareto improvements to the consenting parties (no person is made worse-off and at least one person is made better-off). Following the groundbreaking analysis of the Swedish economist Knut Wicksell (1994) that was described in Chapter 1, Buchanan has argued that in order to be legitimate, constitutional-level political agreements must likewise have the unanimous consent of participants and supply Pareto improvements. Constitutional agreement must be unanimous for the simple reason that an individual cannot involuntarily enter into a social contract; a non-unanimous constitutional agreement would be one that was involuntarily imposed upon some 'contracting' parties.

In constitutional decision-making, it is argued, 'there is *no* place for majority rule or, indeed, for any rule short of unanimity' (CCC, p. 220; See also CoC, in particular Chapter 7; LoL, in particular Chapter 3).

An objection that might be levelled at the approach of constitutional political economy is that, in practice, unanimous agreement is likely to be close to impossible to achieve. At the very least, the requirement of unanimity would seem to assign each individual the power of veto over collective decisions, thereby enabling a small number of recalcitrant individuals or a narrow interest group to impose substantial costs on others as the price of their consent.

Buchanan has argued, however, that there are good reasons to believe that individuals will not use their bargaining power in this way. First, the threat of exclusion from political society will present a powerful incentive to enter into political agreement. Those individuals who remain outside a social contract will not enjoy the protection of the state and may not be able to engage in economic exchanges with others if their property rights are not recognized as legitimate. Hence, the strongest bargaining position may in fact be held by the accommodating collective rather than the recalcitrant individual (LoL, pp. 50–55).

Second, Brennan and Buchanan have pointed out that the fact that any agreement has to be applicable and acceptable to all members of society significantly minimizes the opportunity for a minority of individuals to seek to craft constitutional rules in their favour. Again, any individual or group that attempts to build special privileges into a constitutional agreement will risk being cast into the wilderness outside the protection of the social contract (RoR, p. 33).

Third, Buchanan has pointed out that constitutional choice must take place under what might be termed a 'veil of uncertainty' not dissimilar to the 'veil of ignorance' that John Rawls argued was a prerequisite of the agreement of a social contract (Rawls, 1971).[2] According to Buchanan, because constitutional agreement involves only general rules, it is uncertain how those rules will affect specific individuals or groups. For example, a dairy farmer may favour government price support for milk, but whether the abolition of political interference with all prices will increase or decrease that farmer's net wealth will be uncertain (RoR, p. 34). It is argued that this uncertainty will incentivize support for constitutional rules that maximize the utility of the general population rather than specific individuals:

> [The individual in constitutional choice] cannot predict with any degree of certainty whether he is more likely to be in a winning or a losing coalition on any specific issue. Therefore, he will assume that occasionally he will be in one group and occasionally in the other. His own self-interest will lead him to choose rules that will maximize the utility of an individual in a series of collective decisions with his own preferences on the separate issues being more or less randomly distributed. (CoC, p. 78)

According to Buchanan, the dynamics of constitutional choice in a genuinely individualist democratic setting logically lead to the unanimous agreement of a social contract that does not discriminate among different individuals or groups but rather sets out only general rules that are equally applicable to all. For this reason, it is argued that 'the purely selfish individual and the purely altruistic individual' would make identical constitutional choices (CoC, p. 96).

Public Goods, the Productive State and Non-Unanimous Decisions

In Buchanan's schema the account of the unanimous agreement of a social contact provides, at the very least, an ideal type against which to judge real world political arrangements: it is possible to ask if people can be conceived to unanimously agree a social contract that guaranteed and enforced the property rights that exist in contemporary societies. If the answer to such a question is 'no', then the legitimacy of those political arrangements may be questioned.

However, in almost any conceivable society there are likely to be strong demands for the state to expand its role beyond protection to a productive role in which the state directly supplies public goods – or supplies good as if they were public goods. This expansion of the remit of the state may complicate matters in terms of Buchanan's model of a legitimate state that acts with the unanimous consent of its citizens to bring about Pareto improvements (DSPG, Chapter 1; CoC, Chapter 5; LoL, Chapter 3).

In particular, Buchanan has argued that whereas constitutional choices may be made under a veil of uncertainty with strong incentives for individuals to reach agreement, this may not be the case when people make decisions about the supply of public goods. In choosing the supply of public goods individuals *will* be able to calculate the net personal benefits of different proposals. If such proposals require unanimous support to succeed, some individuals may judge that they stand to benefit by strategically vetoing a proposal for the public supply of a good or service (even if they will be net beneficiaries) on the basis that they can then free-ride on its private provision (and receive an even greater net gain):

> [T]he nature of the unanimity rule is such that group decisions are impossible unless *all* persons agree. A single negative vote blocks a proposal, even if all others in the group approve it. To the extent that participants fully appreciate their own individual blocking power, some negative votes could be predicted with almost any conceivable proposal that might be put forward, regardless of the net benefits provided to each person and regardless of symmetry or fairness properties. Practically speaking, the rule of unanimity would result in few, if any, decisions being made. (DSPG, p. 90)

Accordingly, Buchanan argued, following Wicksell, that if the state is going to be a means via which people overcome public good and free-riding problems, it is necessary to allow for the agreement of some departure from unanimity in post-constitutional political decision-making.

Indeed, Buchanan and Tullock (CoC, p. 81) contended that it would be irrational for a choosing individual to demand that all political decisions be unanimous given the decision-making stasis that this would in all probability create. Rather, the principle of constitutionalism implies the existence of different levels of political decision-making at which different levels of agreement are required. It is the role of the (unanimously agreed) constitution to specify which decision-making rules should apply to different collective decisions below the level of constitutional choice.

In *The Calculus of Consent* Buchanan and Tullock analyzed the costs involved in different decision-making rules. First, all non-unanimous decision-making rules impose *external costs* (i.e. externalities) on those forced to abide by a decision that they do not support. The lower the decision-making threshold, the higher the possible external costs. Second, all decision-making rules have *decision-making costs* that reflect the difficulty of reaching agreement at different thresholds. Unanimity has zero external costs, but potentially very high decision-making costs, whereas simple majority rule produces the inverse: potentially very high external costs but relatively low decision-making costs.

Buchanan and Tullock claimed that there was no theoretical, ethical or other logical reason for believing that simple majority rule, the decision-making rule most closely associated with contemporary democratic practice, had any special properties. Rather, they argued that simple majority rule 'seems, a priori, to represent nothing more than one among the many possible rules' and that 'it would seem very improbable that this rule should be "ideally" chosen for more than a very limited set of collective activities' (CoC, p. 82).

If simple majority rule does have a unique characteristic, it is the potential to impose the highest external costs of any democratic decision-making rule. A decision taken on the basis of the support of half the population plus one $(n/2 + 1)$ imposes external costs on half the population minus one $(n/2 - 1)$. Any qualified majority voting rule reduces the maximum proportion of the population that can suffer the imposition of external costs (of course, this measure of external costs does not take into account intensity of support or opposition to a proposal). Given the potential for very high external costs to be imposed by decisions taken under simple majority rule, a rational individual choosing from all possible decision-making rules would seem to be very unlikely to select this to be the one rule to determine all political decisions (CoC, particularly Chapters 7, 10, 11 and 17).

Buchanan does not propose an ideal voting rule that should be adopted in post-constitutional collective decision-making; such a proposal would assume reference to a scale of values beyond those held by individual men and women. Rather, Buchanan argues that logic suggests that in a moment of constitutional choice people are likely to agree different voting rules for different decisions, depending on the nature of the decision being made and the size of the decision-making group (given that decision-making costs increase as the size of the group increases). It seems reasonable to presume that people will wish to agree upon higher decision-making thresholds for more contentious decisions, mediated to some extent by the size of the relevant population (CoC, Part III; PPNI, Chapter 2).

According to Buchanan, then, the problems of anarchy lead rational individuals to enter into a social contract in which they agree to surrender some of their freedom in return for the protection of property rights guaranteed by the state. The social contract is effectively a political constitution that sets out the 'rules of the game' that are unanimously agreed to govern the political realm. Among these rules of the game will be the decision-making rules that will determine the supply of public goods (and goods supplied as if they were public goods) by the productive state. The high decision-making costs of unanimity and the high external costs of simple majority rule mean that rational individuals are likely to prefer some form(s) of qualified majority voting for lower-level political decisions.

This account provides a justificatory model of constitutional democracy that describes the transition from the protective to the productive state, and from unanimous to non-unanimous decision-making rules, and serves as a benchmark for the evaluation of contemporary democratic practice.

Constitutional Democracy: Procedural not Substantive

For Buchanan, the theoretical foundation of democracy is the unanimous agreement of individuals to enter into a contract that imposes mutual constraints on their behaviour so that they can attain ends that they consider more valuable than the freedom they have relinquished (LoL, Chapter 1; RoR, Chapter 3; PPNI, Chapters 1 and 2).

Buchanan's contractarian approach is neutral with regard to the ends that may be pursued within, or the outcomes that may emerge from, democratic processes:

> [In the contractarian-constitutionalist position] there is no means of evaluating any end state, because there is no external standard or scale through which end states can be 'valued.' End states must be evaluated only through the processes that generate them. What emerges from a process is what emerges and nothing more. If the process is such that individuals seem to be allowed to give due and unbiased expression to *their own values*, however these may be formed and influenced, the results must be deemed acceptable. (RoR, p. 51)

In a democracy, then, individuals will use the political process to pursue whatever ends they happen to judge worthy of pursuit, in the same way that in the economic marketplace individuals will engage in consumption and production decisions in the pursuit of ends that they happen to consider valuable. For Buchanan, democratic politics must be empty of substantive content: democracy describes a set of procedures through which individuals pursue their ends, but it says nothing about what those ends should be.

It should be emphasized, however, that it does not follow that in the contractarian vision individuals may use the political process to do whatever they wish irrespective of the consequences for others. On the contrary, the constitutional constraints agreed in the social contract prohibit individuals from infringing the property rights of others via political (or economic) processes and as such impose limits on what individuals may legitimately do (LoL, Chapter 1; RoR, Chapter 3; PPNI, Chapters 1 and 2).

Buchanan has frequently contrasted his individualist-contractarian-constitutionalist-democratic vision of politics with the view that sees politics as a process of 'truth-discovery' through which the 'common good', 'general interest' or 'social welfare' is to be ascertained and then pursued (e.g. LoL, pp. 20–21; RoR, pp. 46–52; PPNI, p. 4). For Buchanan, this view, which is at the heart of socialist and social democratic conceptions of politics, evaluates political arrangements in terms of the substantive outcomes produced and for this reason it is inherently anti- democratic. In this 'truth-discovery' model of politics, we do not ask if political arrangements effectively enable people to pursue their own self-conceived ends, whatever those ends might be, but ask if 'good' policies have been selected that might in some way move 'society' closer to the realization of some 'common good'. Such an approach is anti-democratic because it refers to values external to those of individual men and women. Accordingly, if government by scientific experts, religious leaders or vocational interests, for example, was found to be the most effective way of determining and pursuing the 'common good', then rule by scientific experts, religious leaders or vocational interests would be logically the most desirable form of government. There is no a priori reason why such a view of politics should lead to the use of democratic procedures in its decision-making processes; if it can be shown that a non-democratic method of decision-making is a more efficient means of discovering what policies are in the 'general interest' then that non-democratic method should logically be adopted (LoL, Chapter 1; RoR, Chapter 3; PPNI, Chapters 1 and 2).

Buchanan argues that the only form of democracy worthy of the name enables individuals to pursue their own self-conceived ends, even if this means that, like the market, democracy frequently produces outcomes that do not meet with the approval of philosophers, politicians or commentators.

The import of this position may be illustrated with an example: between 2001 and 2007 Apple sold 100 million iPod MP3 players worldwide.[3] Accordingly, the consumption decisions of many millions of individuals resulted in the allocation of billions of dollars of economic resources to the production of MP3 players. Some people might judge this to be a frivolous, wasteful or even immoral use of those resources compared to other possible uses, such as poverty reduction, education provision or healthcare supply. But even in contemporary democracies it is generally judged that the relevant decision calculus is that of the individual who chooses whether or not to purchase an MP3 player; the purchase of an MP3 player does not (yet) require political approval based on the evaluation of the social outcomes produced by such consumption decisions.

Buchanan applies the same principle to the political realm: individuals may choose to use political processes to pursue what some might consider similarly frivolous, wasteful or even immoral ends. As in the economic realm the relevant decision calculus is that of the choosing individual, so that whatever outcomes happen to be produced are of no concern to others (as long as their property rights are not infringed). From Buchanan's perspective, if democracy is founded upon the notion of individual sovereignty then there is no reason to believe that different evaluative standards should apply in the economic and the political realms; the relevant decision calculus in both cases must be the choosing individual.

In reading Buchanan's critique of political processes in contemporary democracies in the following section, it is important to bear in mind the normative commitment to democracy at the heart of Buchanan's work. Buchanan's public choice theory is extremely critical of the workings of contemporary democracies, but this is not a critique of democracy as an ideal or a principle. Rather, Buchanan offers a critique of the misuse and perversion of democracy. In particular, according to Buchanan, the label of democracy has been used to provide legitimacy to political activities that are inherently undemocratic.

The Problems of Non-Contractarian Politics: Re-Entering Anarchy

Buchanan has written that the contemporary United States of America may be described as a 'constitutional anarchy':

a society 'where the range and extent of federal government influence over individual behavior depend largely on the accidental preferences of politicians in judicial, legislative, and executive positions of power' (LoL, p. 19). It is a society where the preferences of elite politicians, not the choices of individual men and women, determine the actions undertaken by the state. Consequently:

> Increasingly, men feel themselves at the mercy of a faceless, irresponsible bureaucracy, subject to unpredictable twists and turns that destroy and distort personal expectations with little opportunity for redress or retribution. (LoL, p. 19)

America may be characterized as a constitutional anarchy because although a constitution ostensibly does exist that sets out and protects the rights of citizens, in reality collective decisions are frequently imposed on individuals without their consent and such decisions often infringe people's basic property rights.

Examples of such infringements would include compulsory taxation to fund programmes or transfers of which people do not approve, prosecution for 'crimes' that do not create third party victims, and subsidies and price controls that amount to transfers of wealth from consumers to special interest groups. It is argued that the state that was created to protect against infringements of liberty now carries out such infringements as a matter of its routine operation.

Although Buchanan's work in this area is written almost exclusively in abstract terms, or very occasionally uses American examples and context, his analysis is nevertheless applicable to all contemporary democracies. This section will present in detail four key dimensions to Buchanan's critique of contemporary democracies as constitutional anarchies. First, it will show the frequent disparities that exist between individual preferences and the choices that emerge from democratic decision-making processes, particularly when simple majority voting rules are used. Second, it will set out the ways in which democratic procedures allow majority or powerful groups to exploit or impose external costs on minorities or less powerful groups. Third, it will set out the problems of political rent-seeking that have become endemic to contemporary democracies. Finally, it will show the problems that arise when the state is granted enormous powers that may make it reminiscent of the spectre of Leviathan that haunts Hobbes's classic work of that title.

Individual preferences and 'democratic' outcomes

Public policies pursued by democratic governments have legitimacy at least in part because they are said to reflect the preferences of individual citizens. Classical mandate theories of representative democracy see democratic choice as a process through which voters select representatives on the basis of the evaluation of alternative policy programmes. It is believed that within this process the manifesto that most closely reflects popular preferences will receive democratic endorsement and then be implemented by the government. At the subsequent election the governing coalition is held accountable for the policies it has implemented and failure to have put into practice 'the will of the people' will result in removal from office. This process incentivizes political parties to move their policies as close to the preferences of the median voter as possible and to implement those policies when in office. It is believed that via this process public policies in democratic countries are broadly aligned with the preferences of individual voters (e.g. McDonald and Budge, 2006).

The notion that the democratic mandate legitimizes the policies introduced by democratic governments has a powerful hold on the popular and scholarly imaginations, so much so that, as Buchanan and Tullock (CoC, p. 83) noted, 'By and large, scholars have assumed, without being conscious of it, that all State action takes place as if there were unanimous consent'. That is, scholars often write about democratic policies as if they reflect the unanimous preferences of the members of a particular society, when very often the *most* that can be claimed for such policies is that they reflect the preferences of a majority of the population. But if different decision-making rules were in place, such as qualified majority voting, very often those policies would not be approved and would therefore not receive the stamp of democratic legitimacy.

Political economists, however, have long been troubled by the relationship between the outcomes of democratic elections and the preferences of individual electors. Such concerns can be traced back at least as far as Condorcet's (1785) mathematical analysis of simple majority voting which proved that when three or more people choose between three or more differently valued alternatives, collective choices become intransitive. That is, when choosing between three alternatives A, B and C, even if the majority of voters prefer A to B and prefer B to C, it is possible for C to be chosen over A in a simple majority voting contest.[4]

Buchanan's contribution to our understanding of the relationship between individual preferences and democratic outcomes has been made in the context of and built upon these earlier works, but it has focused upon the analysis of the specific characteristics of democratic processes and practices that can distort and misrepresent individual preferences.

Buchanan and Tullock's *The Calculus of Consent* highlighted the fact that – holding individual preferences constant – different voting rules will produce different outcomes. This point can be illustrated by adapting a simple example from that book (p. 122): consider a five-person group that has to vote once to decide how to divide up the one and only lot of manna that has fallen from heaven. If the decision is made by a simple majority rule, the first three individuals to form a voting coalition will secure control of the manna. However, if a qualified majority voting rule imposing a threshold of two-thirds of the population is introduced, a fourth member of the coalition is required to secure control of the manna. Although both outcomes would generally be considered 'democratic', and therefore a legitimate representation of the preferences of the group members, there is in fact a qualitative difference between the two outcomes for the group members: one outcome gives control of the manna to three people, the other outcome allocates control to four; different voting rules produce different outcomes from the same population with the same preferences.[5]

For Buchanan, of course, the fact that the use of different voting rules by a single population may produce different outcomes does not render those outcomes illegitimate. On the contrary, for Buchanan outcomes can only acquire legitimacy from the fact that they have arisen as a consequence of the operation of rules agreed by the participants: it is unanimously agreed rules that give legitimacy to outcomes, not vice versa (RoR, Chapters 7 and 8). However, the impact of different voting rules on outcomes may provide evidence of the often arbitrary nature of the relationship between individual preferences and public policies in contemporary democracies, something that should give cause for reflection to those who would romanticize democratically chosen public policies as always representing 'the will of the people'.

Furthermore, Buchanan has set out a number of characteristics of majoritarian democratic procedures that may create a disparity between individual preferences and the public policies chosen via democratic decision-making. Some of these factors may be mutually exclusive and therefore the impact may be relatively limited, but other factors may be mutually reinforcing and here the combined or cumulative impact may be more profound. The characteristics of majoritarian democratic procedures that create such problems may become particularly apparent when individual decision-making in politics and markets are compared – it can be seen that the notion that voter sovereignty may be in some way analogous, or even superior, to consumer sovereignty may be seriously flawed.

The first such characteristic is the frequently *exclusive* nature of political choices. In the economic marketplace, production and consumption decisions are made at the margin: consumers will choose whether to purchase an additional unit of a good or service at a particular cost price and producers will similarly decide whether to supply an additional unit of a good or service at a particular sale price. By contrast, as Buchanan has noted, 'politics differs categorically from markets in that, in political competition, there are mutually exclusive sets of winners and losers' (LFCL, p. 56). Some goods and services, by their very nature, cannot be supplied in marginal units. A new motorway, for example, cannot be purchased in marginal units but must either be built or not built. The supply of a good or service in the political realm, however, frequently gives it these exclusive, all-or-nothing, characteristics from the perspective of the individual. An individual in receipt of government-provided healthcare, for example, does not have the option to pay marginally more for a marginally higher standard of provision or to pay marginally less for a marginally lower standard.

Political decisions, then, may not be equivalent to a decision among roommates on the setting of a thermostat in their sleeping quarters, so that a median point will be selected that broadly satisfies all participants. Rather, political decisions may be more analogous to the decision as to whether or not a nation should go to war, with each alternative being highly unpalatable to those who favour the other (LFCL, pp. 55–56; PFDP, Chapter 2; PPNI, Chapter 5).

The second factor that may create a disparity between individual preferences and the outcomes of democratic decision-making processes is the *miniscule influence of any individual vote* in contemporary democratic practices. Put simply, as Vanberg and Buchanan described: 'the impact on the outcome [of an election] of any and every vote is $1/n$' (CCC, p. 132n). That is, the impact of any and every vote is one divided by the total number of votes cast. Any changes to a single individual's preferences will therefore almost certainly have no bearing on the outcome of an election. Thus, if one voter in a US presidential election switches his or her vote from the Democrats to the Republicans, or vice versa, perhaps after four years of soul-searching and intense deliberation, that change of allegiance will make no difference whatsoever to the outcome of the election. Consequently, as Brennan and Buchanan have explained, 'a major difference emerges' between how individuals approach public and private choices, 'when the individual recognizes that, for public or collective choice, the possible changes in his own preferences may be irrelevant' (RoR, p. 85).

In the classic public choice account developed in particular by Downs (1957), the fact that individuals do not cast decisive ballots means that the costs of individual investment in political information-gathering are likely to exceed the benefits. Rational individuals, therefore, will not invest in costly information-gathering about the candidates and parties contesting an election. In the words of Vanberg and Buchanan:

> The specific, and limited, claim is that in a large constituency (with a secret ballot), the impact of a single vote on the outcome is insignificant; therefore, the prospects of an individual's improving the outcome by casting a single better informed vote do not provide significant incentives for a voter to incur the costs of becoming better informed, even if these costs are quite small. (CCC, p. 132)

It is claimed that the incentives that the vast majority of individuals encounter in the political realm lead them to choose to remain 'rationally ignorant' of policy and politics. If people are not informed about politics, they may effectively delegate political decision-making to elite actors for whom information-gathering is a rational choice – for politicians and aspirant politicians it will make sense to be informed about politics. Elections then become a choice, made by relatively uninformed voters, between elite actors who will take political decisions on behalf of the majority of the population. According to Vanberg and Buchanan, the difference between decision-making in political and economic contexts may be analogous to 'the difference between a choice among experts themselves and a choice among their products' (CCC, p. 137; See also: PT, pp. 24–25; MSMO, pp. 62–63).

Writing in the context of constitutional choice, although their analysis applies equally to post-constitutional political decision-making, Vanberg and Buchanan have used the analogy of the manufacture of cars to illustrate the consequences of the delegation of political choice to elite actors. In contemporary markets, the choice between different (expert-produced) cars 'can be done reliably with little knowledge of the technical expertise that actually lies behind production'; most people are able to purchase a car that they consider satisfactory without any knowledge of how the car was made or how it functions. But if consumers are required to choose one automobile manufacturer that is to be given the exclusive right to supply all cars for a specified period, 'the informational requirement for an intelligent choice would be significantly higher'. In this scenario, people are required to make a much more complicated judgement about the relative technical competence of different experts and the likely performance of their proposed automobiles. It seems reasonable to posit that individuals are much more likely to be able to obtain a car that reflects their preferences when they choose between cars produced by experts than when they choose between experts to produce cars (CCC, p. 138).

It is for this reason that the miniscule influence of any single vote in democratic elections and the widespread rational ignorance that follows from this leads to a disparity between individual preferences and public policies: in the political realm individuals will select 'experts' who are in fact unable to produce the goods and services that people wish to consume.

The third characteristic of majoritarian democracy that may lead to a disparity between individual preferences and policy outcomes is the high degree of *uncertainty* that confronts participants in democratic decision-making. Democratic decision-makers face a degree of uncertainty not present in other decision-making contexts because of the hiatus between their choice and the final outcome. As Buchanan and Tullock wrote:

> In analyzing the behavior of the individual in the political process, there is an important element of uncertainty present that cannot be left out of account. No longer is there the one-to-one correspondence between individual choice and final action. In the case of any specific decision-making rule for the group, the individual participant has no way of knowing the final outcome, the social choice, at the time he makes his own contribution to this outcome. (CoC, p. 37)

Hence, whereas in the marketplace an individual's decision to purchase a house, a car or a cup of coffee, for example, means that they will acquire ownership of that good, in the political realm an individual's decision to choose (i.e. vote for) a particular policy programme does not necessarily mean that the programme will be implemented. Rather, the outcome is dependent upon the votes of the other participants in the decision-making process, which cannot be predicted with absolute certainty, and then on the implementation of the chosen policies by politicians and bureaucrats, which similarly cannot be guaranteed with absolute certainly.

In one of his earliest papers, Buchanan argued that the uncertainty inherent to political decision-making 'must influence to some degree the behavior of the individual in choosing among the possible social alternatives offered to him' (LFCL, p. 77). Rather than simply selecting their most-preferred option, a participant in political decision-making may try to anticipate the choices of other participants and for this reason decide to strategically vote for second-best or least-worst alternatives if these options are believed to have a greater prospect of electoral success than the most-preferred alternative. Uncertainty, then, may lead individual choices to become intransitive; individuals who prefer A to B and B to C, may choose to vote for C in preference to A, if they believe that option C has more chance of defeating the least-desirable alternative, which we may term option D (LFCL, p. 77; CoC, pp. 37–38).[6]

Buchanan has argued that uncertainty may also exist in democratic decision-making with regard to the distribution of benefits and burdens that result from political decisions. Whereas a private choice that an individual makes in the economic marketplace will lead to direct and comparatively easy to estimate costs and benefits, the same cannot necessarily be said of choices made in the political realm. If an individual buys a house, car or cup of coffee in the marketplace, for example, the personal costs will be the monetary price of the good purchased, while the benefits will be the anticipated individual utility derived from that good. But if an individual votes for a particular public healthcare programme, education policy or defence system, even if the selected policy is electorally successful, it may not necessarily be clear in advance where the costs and benefits will fall. As Buchanan and Tullock noted: 'The chooser-voter will, of course, recognize the existence of both the benefit and the cost side of any proposed public action, but neither his own share in the benefits nor his own share in the costs can be so readily estimated as in the comparable market choices' (CoC, p. 38).

Furthermore, Buchanan has argued that the uncertain distribution of benefits and burdens in the political realm may be heightened by the presence of complex fiscal institutions and progressive rates of direct taxation. A taxpayer may judge that at current levels of public and private expenditure he or she would be willing to support higher levels of public expenditure to fund the provision of a particular public good. As a result of progressive income tax rates or levels of indirect taxation that fall disproportionately on particular consumption patterns, however, it may be that the burden of the extra public expenditure falls so excessively on that particular individual that he or she would in fact not support the additional expenditure in the light of the new distribution of benefits and burdens that its supply would produce. But in the context of fiscal complexity that new distribution of benefits and burdens may not be apparent to the taxpayer-voter until after the voting event has taken place and the new or increased taxes required to pay for the supply of the good have been levied.

In the political realm, then, individuals may make choices that they would not make if they knew with certainty the post-decision distribution of costs and benefits. For Buchanan, this adds further weight to the contention that in democratic processes individuals 'may be led by the structure of the institutions to choose nonoptimally or inefficiently' (PFDP, p. 42). As Buchanan and Tullock concluded:

> For these reasons . . . we should not expect models based on the assumption of rational individual behavior to yield as fruitful a result when applied to collective-choice processes as similar models have done when applied to market or economic choices. (CoC, p. 39)

It is argued, then, that in the political arena individuals may make choices that do not accord with their self-conceived ends and/or their personal preferences may be translated into outcomes that have intransitive qualities.

Buchanan has argued that the *temporal* dimension of political decision-making may further separate individual preferences from collective outcomes. In any choosing situation, an individual may face a choice between the attainment of short-term and long-term ends. For example, a person may have to choose between using their disposable income for short-term consumption, such as the purchase of new clothes, and using it for long-term investment, such as the reduction of their mortgage liabilities.

When making a private choice, like the example above, an individual knows that, ceteris paribus, the decision to save for the future will result in increased future income. In a public choice setting, however, the uncertainty surrounding the choices that other people may make means that a decision to save for the future may not necessarily result in increased future income. On the contrary, an individual's decision to forgo present consumption may mean that the income they thought they had saved for the future is consumed by others either now or in the future.

For example, an individual may choose not to support a plan to build a new road, even though the anticipated personal benefits of the road exceed the anticipated personal costs, because he or she believes that delaying construction for a number of years will enable the road to be built in a more favourable economic climate. However, if the road building is postponed, the resources saved may be allocated to other public expenditure projects that the choosing individual values less highly. If the individual anticipates this outcome, it will be logical for him or her to support the immediate construction of the road, even though this is not the alternative he or she would select in a private context. In the words of Brennan and Buchanan, in a public choice setting, 'The individual will tend to make voting choices in terms of a shorter time horizon than that reflected in his private choices' (RoR, p. 86). The shorter time horizon utilized in public, rather than private, choices further divides individual preferences from collective outcomes.

A fifth factor that may drive a wedge between individual preferences and collective outcomes identified by Buchanan is the fact that political choices may be *uncosted* when they are presented to the choosing public. In contemporary democratic polities, the costs and benefits of public policies tend to be treated entirely separately. In the absence of earmarked taxes it will be extremely rare for specific costs to be attached to specific policies or for individual taxpayers to be able to accurately estimate the costs of specific proposals. Rather, on one side of the balance sheet individuals will be asked to approve or reject proposals for public expenditure divorced from questions of fiscal policy, while on the other side of the ledger individuals will be asked to vote for proposals to levy given amounts of taxation similarly divorced from the expenditure proposals that the taxes will be used to fund (PFDP, pp. 90–92).

Furthermore, where a large proportion of public expenditure is financed via the creation of public debt then it may indeed be the case that public expenditure can be funded at no cost to the choosing taxpayer. Buchanan has cited the funding of the US federal space program in the 1960s via public borrowing as an example of this phenomenon:

> If the individual citizen were asked, in mid-1963, his opinions on proposed expansions in the federal space program, he could, roughly and in some fashion, measure benefits in terms of sport, national prestige, adventure, technological fallout, etc. But what were the costs?

He would not have translated the costs of the space program into increased taxes. And for a very simple reason: the individual knew that he would not have to pay such taxes. The predictable result of a democratic choice process is the generation of budget deficits when borrowing is available as an alternative to taxation unless deficit creation is not somehow restrained by constitutional limitations. (PFDP, p. 102)

The US space program, then, was financed via increased government borrowing, meaning that contemporary taxpayers were not required to pay extra taxes to fund the programme. Rather, the cost was deferred to future taxpayers who would inherit responsibility for repaying government debt.

Where public spending can be funded via increased public borrowing, and the burden of present consumption can thereby be passed on to future generations, it will be logical for individual voters to choose to increase public expenditure at no extra cost to themselves. Indeed, it is hard to imagine why an individual would not select this course of action when such an alternative is available, especially if it is presented to the voting public as a means of funding present consumption that has long-term benefits, thus helping to overcome people's moral inhibitions about imposing such costs on future generations (PPPD, Chapters 1–6 and 12; PFDP, Chapters 7 and 8).

The separation of costs and benefits in political decision-making could appear to provide evidence of a strong correlation between individual preferences and public policies given that it would seem to show that decision-making in political processes can lead to a large number of people's favoured expenditure proposals to be realized simultaneously. Such a conclusion would be mistaken, however, because individual preferences properly understood reflect people's evaluation of the relative costs and benefits of different courses of action, rather than an infinite wish list of goods and services that would be consumed if such consumption were costless. By offering seemingly costless consumption the political process in fact creates a disparity between what people would choose if they were fully cognizant of the relevant costs and benefits and the choices people make in the political realm. As such, this analysis provides another example of how the political process can lead people to make choices that do not reflect their genuine preferences that would emerge if and when they were fully informed of the relevant costs and benefits of the alternatives.

A sixth factor that may produce a disparity between individual preferences and the policy outcomes that result from collective choice is the *bundling* of goods and services in the political realm. In the marketplace, an individual is faced with the choice of a wide range of goods and services. Here, 'If an individual desires *more* of a particular commodity or service, the market normally requires only that he take *less* of another commodity or service' (LFCL, p. 81). In the marketplace, an individual is able to select a bespoke consumption bundle that will reflect his or her relative valuation of different goods and services. In the political realm, however, 'few voting schemes include means which enable an individual to break down his total voting strength into fractional parts' (LFCL, p. 81). Consequently, in making an electoral choice an individual will be required to vote for the package of goods and services that most closely corresponds with his or her preferences, but it is highly probable that all the goods and services in the selected package will be under- or over-supplied relative to the quantities the choosing individual would select if each good and service was purchased discretely (PFDP, Chapter 6).

It may be objected that bundling similarly takes place in the marketplace. There is indeed some truth in this objection: it is impossible to purchase most newspapers without the sports section, so that newspaper readers with no interest in sports will have to pay for a section of their newspaper that he or she has no wish to read. However, the bundles that exist in the political realm are of a different magnitude compared to those that exist in the economic sphere. In a contemporary democracy an individual must choose between expenditure plans that can constitute a third to a half of a country's GDP – a choice that bares little comparison to the bundles that exist in private markets.

The fact that voters must select bundles of goods and services almost inevitably leads them to make choices some way removed from the genuine preferences that would be revealed if they purchased the same goods and services in the marketplace. As noted above, for example, in voting for a package of goods and services an individual will almost certainly give approval to the under- and over-supply of goods and services relative to the quantities that would be selected if they chose discretely. Similarly, an individual who supports all of a candidate's policies bar one, perhaps the candidate's education policy, may choose to vote for that candidate as the least-worst alternative, but by so doing the voter is deemed to give his or her assent to the candidate's education policy, even though it does not reflect his or her own preferences. In this way in the political realm, individuals are led to vote for policies that are contrary to their own preferences.

The seventh factor identified by Buchanan that may lead to a disparity between individual preferences and policy outcomes is the failure of voting rules to take into account the different *intensity* of people's preferences. Put simply, standard one-person, one-vote rules mean that 'even those voters who are completely indifferent on a given issue will find their preferences given as much weight as those of the most concerned individuals' (CoC, p. 134). This situation may be contrasted with choice in economic markets where individuals possess multiple dollars, which may be characterized as multiple 'votes', that can be used to secure the production of the goods and services that they value most highly, even if very few of their fellow citizens similarly value those products (LFCL, pp. 82–88).

Buchanan and Tullock (CoC, pp. 127–128) developed a formal model to show how the failure of political processes to weight preferences effectively can lead to sub-optimal outcomes that do not accurately reflect individual preferences. Buchanan and Tullock presented an example in which an electorate must choose between two alternatives where 51 per cent of voters favour option A and 49 per cent of voters favour option B. First, suppose that the positive and negative intensities of preferences are equal. This equal intensity may be interpreted to indicate that any voter would be willing to give up his preference (to accept B when he or she prefers A) for $100. Thus, where intensities of preference are equal, 'passage of the legislation in question will benefit 51 per cent of the voters by $100 each, and it will harm 49 per cent of the voters by $100 each', so that, 'In the hundred-man model, A would be selected by simple majority voting, and total benefits of $5100 exceed total losses of $4900' (CoC, p. 127).

If individual intensities of preference are not equal over all voters, however, a different picture will emerge. Assume, for example, that those who favour A will be willing to give up their preference for $50 and those who favour B remain willing to give up their preference for $100. Assuming the same 51 per cent to 49 per cent division between those favouring A and those favouring B, simple majority voting will produce the same outcome of majority support for A, but now the total benefits of $2550 are exceeded by total losses of $4900. Hence, once intensity of preference is taken into account, it can be demonstrated that a simple choice between two alternatives, conducted according to simple majority rule, can produce an outcome that does not reflect individual preferences and is welfare-reducing.[7]

Buchanan and Tullock (CoC, p. 134) noted that in this context popular acceptance of the contention that people have a duty to vote is likely to weaken rather than strengthen the ability of democratic processes to accurately reflect voter preferences. If people vote out of a sense of duty, rather than from a strong desire to see a particular policy outcome triumph at the polls, then the votes of people who are relatively sanguine about the outcome of an election are likely to crowd out the votes of people who care passionately about the result. In such a situation, ceteris paribus, the more intensely held preferences of a minority may be defeated by the less intensely held preferences of a majority, producing a sub-optimal outcome akin to the one set out in the formal model above.[8]

At the centre of Buchanan's intellectual contribution, then, is an account of the ways in which contemporary democratic decision-making distorts and skewers individual preferences, frequently leading individuals' choices to assume intransitive characteristics and producing outcomes that are inconsistent with the preferences of individual voter-choosers. This aspect of Buchanan's work, then, contains a systematic account of endemic failure within the political process.

This section will now turn to Buchanan's account of the ways in which contemporary democratic processes may allow some individuals to exploit, or – to use less emotive language – impose external costs on, others.

Exploitation or the imposition of external costs

For Buchanan, a fundamental distinction between politics and markets is the existence of an exit option in market relationships that is absent from politics: if an individual does not wish to purchase a good or service in the marketplace, then he or she may choose to exit from that transaction, whereas in the political realm individuals must contribute to the supply of collectively provided goods and services or face legal penalty. As Buchanan has put it: 'In its stylized form, the market involves no coercion, no extraction of value from any participant without consent. In dramatic contrast, politics is inherently coercive, independent of the effective decision rules that may be operative' (FFL, p. 69).

Because politics does not have an exit option comparable to that found in the market, there is an inherent potential for political institutions to be used by one group to exploit others. The essence of majority rule is the rule of one group, the majority, over another, the minority: 'By its nature, majority rule means that the minority is ruled, is coerced into acceptance of states of affairs that its members do not prefer' (PPC, p. 91). Or as Buchanan and Congleton simply put it: 'majority rule means that members of the minority are ruled' (PPNI, p. 69).

Buchanan has argued that because, as described in the previous section, political decisions tend to be exclusive either/or decisions, rather than more/less decisions where compromise may be easily attainable, voting under majority rule tends not to produce outcomes close to median preferences. Rather, 'majoritarian equilibria' tend to be where the majority imposes their preferences on minorities (PPC, pp. 90–111; PPNI, p. 69).

Buchanan's work provides a compelling account of how individuals seeking to escape the wretchedness of the state of nature, where every individual is at constant risk of predatory attack, find themselves locked into a political structure where the risk of predatory exploitation is similarly ever present.

In Buchanan's contractarian scheme set out earlier in this chapter, it is in each individual's self-interest to enter into the social contract and receive the benefits of the protective state. The protective state has theoretical legitimacy because it is founded upon the unanimous consent of the contracting parties. To overcome the difficulties of efficiently supplying public goods and the high decision-making costs associated with unanimous agreement, contracting individuals may also agree to supply some public goods in the political realm and to use non-unanimous decision-making rules for these post-constitutional choices.

As set out in the previous section, however, the vagaries of real world political decision-making mean that it is very unlikely that the quantity of public goods supplied will correspond to the quantity demanded by any individual citizen. Consequently:

> [T]he average or representative citizen must anticipate that he will rarely, if ever, optimally prefer the particular budgetary package that he will be required to enjoy and to pay for. Given almost any budgetary package, the citizen must expect that he would prefer expansion in some items, contractions in others, even within the same revenue constraint. And, overall, he may prefer that the

total outlay be larger or smaller than that to which he is subjected. (LoL, pp. 130–131)

In such a situation, there is an inherent pull towards budgetary expansion as many different individuals seek to remedy the under-supply of some publicly supplied goods and services, whereas individuals may be less motivated to seek to correct over-supply because having too much of a good or service may be less pressing than having too little (PFDP, Chapter 6). However, as the size and scope of government grows relative to the private sector of the economy, the individual citizen's level of dissatisfaction with the goods and services he is required to purchase via compulsory taxation must also grow, because he or she is required to purchase more and more goods at quantities that do not correspond with his or her own preferences. In this scenario, in order '[t]o enforce its decisions, the productive state must call on its complement, the protective state' (LoL, p. 131).

An individual who would voluntarily enter into the social contract to ensure that his or her rights are protected, and would likewise voluntarily agree to the creation of the productive state to overcome the collective action problems that inhibit the supply of public goods, may nevertheless find themselves forced to pay for goods and services that they do not wish to consume, and if an attempt is made to refuse or avoid payment they may then find themselves exposed to the force of the protective state:

> He is forced to abide by choices made for him by others, which may involve a net reduction in his own command over material goods. Taxes are levied on him, without his consent, to finance goods and services that he may value less highly than the foregone private-goods alternatives.

The activity of the enforcing agent becomes quite different here than it is with reference to ordinary contractual agreements among separate parties. (LoL, pp. 131–132)

In such a situation, then, the individual citizen is returned to what amounts to a state of anarchy, where they are constantly threatened with predation and their rights may be summarily dismissed: 'To the individual citizen who may oppose a particular outcome, enforcement here is not one whit different from exogenous destruction in his rights' (LoL, p. 131).

Moreover, where the belief that majority rule equates to 'democracy' legitimizes whatever decision the majority happens to make, there are no limits to what decisions can be made, what property may be taken and what rights may be destroyed. As Buchanan and Congleton stated:

So long as political actions are determined by majoritarian coalitions, there are no grounds for complaint or concern on behalf of those persons or groups who may be differentially exploited. There is, indeed, no constitutionally protected sphere of activity into which politics cannot potentially enter. In essence, majoritarian agreement is the ultimate source of value. All and everything are politicizable. (PPNI, p. 25)

A similar account of the inherent dangers of majority rule was given by Buchanan and Tullock in *The Calculus of Consent*:

[T]he existence of such external costs [costs imposed on the individual by collective action] is inherent in the operation of any collective decision-making rule other than that of unanimity. Indeed, the essence of the collective-choice process under majority voting rules is the fact that the minority of voters are forced to accede to actions which they cannot prevent and for which they cannot claim compensation for damages resulting. (CoC, p. 89)

It is argued, then, that although people may contract in to the state to escape the constant threat of predation in the state of nature, the expansion of the remit of the state to include the provision of public goods chosen via simple majority rule leads to a situation where every individual is liable to have costs imposed upon him or her by others without opportunity for redress.

According to Buchanan, the ease with which majoritarian processes can be used to force people to pay for benefits that others receive leads inexorably to the development of the welfare state, where income and wealth are redistributed without any pretence of overcoming the free-rider problems associated with the supply of public goods (PPNI, Chapter 2).

In the context of the redistributive state, politics becomes a blatant means of *taking* other people's property: the Hobbesian war of all against all that people sought sanctuary from in the social contract, 'is simply transferred to the realm of institutionally organized conflict', so that 'politics is a continuation of war by other means' (PPNI, p. 25). In the political realm, then, people re-enter the bleak anarchical situation where their rights are constantly threatened and predation is ever present. The political process becomes the mechanism by which different groups compete to be the winners and losers in the economic transfer game.

Although the welfare state may be often justified in terms of 'distributive justice', there is in fact no guarantee that the poor will be members of the dominant majority that benefits from a system of transfer payments. On the contrary, given the costs of political mobilization there are good reasons to believe that the poor will very often not be members of the dominant voting majority. In reality, redistribution via the welfare state may often involve the exploitation of the poorest members of society by the relatively wealthy majority: 'The implementation of political transfers will always be such that the direction of transfer is away from the minority and toward the decisive majority, and the poorest cannot be expected to be in the decisive majority any more often than anyone else' (RoR, p. 142).[9]

The political process may also be used as a mechanism for the exploitation of one group by another when public expenditure is financed via the creation of public debt. In *Public Principles of Public Debt*, Buchanan argued that public expenditure funded via public borrowing involves the present generation of taxpayers imposing the costs of current expenditure on future generations of taxpayers. If money sourced from public debt is invested in projects with long-term benefits, for example in the construction of a bridge that creates cost savings into the future, then future generations may benefit from the expenditure that they fund. But if that money is consumed without regard to the long-term, for example to fund a celebration marking a particular national anniversary, then a burden is imposed on future generations who have enjoyed no linked benefit.

But irrespective of whether such money is invested wisely or wasted, it nevertheless remains the case that, 'the real cost of public expenditure which is debt financed must rest on individuals *other* than those who participate in the decisions made at the time of the approval or rejection of any proposed expenditure' (PPPD, p. 119). Hence, when public spending decisions are made now but paid for later, by definition those who pay must be different individuals from those who choose.

Moreover, as noted in the previous section, where present benefits may be funded via public debt creation, it will be logical for individual voters to prefer to finance public expenditure via this method which transfers the costs to future taxpayers. We should, therefore, expect to see rising public debt burdens in democratic states – as has indeed been the case in all contemporary democracies (PPPD, particularly Chapter 12; PFDP, Chapters 7 and 8).

It is not only majorities who are able to use democratic processes to impose costs on minorities or future taxpayers, however. When the standard workings of representative democracy are factored into the analysis, the exploitative potential of democracy becomes even greater because in a representative democracy a *minority* of voters are often able to control the decision-making process.

In *The Calculus of Consent*, Buchanan and Tullock (CoC, Chapter 15) demonstrated the ability of minorities to dominate representative democratic institutions with a simple model of a polity of 25 voters who organize themselves into five constituencies of five people for the purpose of appointing representatives to conduct their mutual affairs. Figure 2.2 below shows that when arranged in five constituencies of five people, nine voters are able to control the decision-making process.

In this model, the three electors highlighted with a cross in each of the constituencies r_1, r_2 and r_3 will elect the representative in their constituency by a winning margin of three votes to two votes, and then their elected representatives will be able to dominate the legislature by a similar margin of three votes to two voters.

This basic model demonstrates the general point that in a representative democracy (including one governed by

	r_1	r_2	r_3	r_4	r_5
	×	×	×		
	×	×	×		
	×	×	×		

Figure 2.2

a bicameral legislature; see CoC, Chapter 16, particularly the model on p. 238) an organized minority of voters will be able to dominate the disorganized majority. Buchanan and Tullock explained that, '[i]n the real world, as the number of voters and constituencies increases, the minimum-sized coalition required for dominance under simple majority voting approaches ¼ of all voters as a limit', so that, for example, if there are 39,601 voters arranged in 199 constituencies of 199 voters each, only 10,000 voters would be required to secure passage of any given policy proposal – only 100 more than one-quarter of all the voters (CoC, p. 220).

The consequences for the evaluation of contemporary representative democracy should be apparent:

> Thus, a logrolling [that is, coalition-forming] bargain to obtain benefits from the political process need only involve about ¼ of the voters under a representative system. Therefore, representative institutions of this type are almost equivalent to permitting any group of

¼ of the voters in direct democracy to form a logrolling coalition empowered to determine what roads will be repaired, which harbors dredged, and which special interest groups will receive government aid . . . it should not be necessary to point out how great the external cost imposed by such a procedure would be. (CoC, p. 220)

Hence, while direct democracy operating under a simple majority rule enables (n/2 + 1) or more of the population to exploit their fellows, under representative democracy, which is of course the norm in contemporary democracies, an organized minority of about a quarter of the population will be able to exploit the majority. This does not necessarily mean that minorities will always be organized so efficiently, or that they will always use their power in a predatory fashion, but it does mean that the potential for such exploitation by minorities will always be present in representative arrangements in the absence of qualified majority voting rules or the constitutional limits on the power of government that will be discussed later in this chapter.

The question arises, then, of how frequently we might expect majorities or minorities to use their political power to exploit other people. It might be objected that Buchanan's analysis presupposes a pessimistic view of human nature which overestimates the willingness of people to engage in predatory action against others. It was shown earlier in this chapter that Buchanan has an ambiguous view of human nature; Buchanan views people as neither irredeemably good nor irredeemably bad, but usually some combination of the two (LoL, Chapter 2; RoR, Chapter 4; WITANAC, Chapter 11). The salient question may be whether different institutional arrangements incentivize good or bad behaviour, or incentivize the recruitment of principally good or bad people to positions of power. Or, as Brennan and Buchanan phrased the question: 'If institutions are such as to permit a selected number of persons to exercise discretionary powers over others, what sort of persons should be predicted to occupy these positions?' (RoR, p. 72).

In an argument that has strong echoes of Hayek's (1944, Chapter 10) account of 'why the worst get on top' in politics, Brennan and Buchanan argued that if political power is understood, using an economic analogy, as a monopoly right that is auctioned to the highest bidder, then we should expect the person willing to pay the most for that monopoly right to be the person who expects to gain the most from it. That person is likely to be the one prepared to exploit it most ruthlessly: 'positions of political power will tend to attract those persons who place higher values on the possession of such power. These persons will tend to be the highest bidders in the allocation of political offices' (RoR, p. 72).

It is argued that people who may seek elected office in order to pursue other-regarding ends may not be sufficiently motivated to invest large amounts of time and effort to win political power, given that such ends may be realized by other people attaining office or by other means, such as work in philanthropic organisations. Those who desire to wield power over others for personal gain, on the other hand, may only be able to realize this end by personally achieving political power, creating a powerful incentive to devote substantial resources to securing elected office (RoR, pp. 72–73).

It will also be the case that the benefits of political power will be greatest for those whose views or preferences are at most variance with the views or preferences of the majority of the population. An individual who desires a social outcome different from the social outcome that most other people would choose is likely to gain most from acquiring the monopoly right to exercise political power. For this reason Brennan and Buchanan argue that it should be expected that 'political institutions will be populated by individuals whose interests will conflict with those of ordinary citizens' (RoR, p. 73).

Here, then, the analysis reinforces Hume's dictum that political institutions should be designed as if every person were a knave with no end other than his or her own private interests, even though not all people behave knavishly (Hume, 1777, p. 44). To design political institutions on the basis that those who hold political power will always be benevolent is to provide enormous scope for the exploitation of the powerless by the powerful (RoR, particularly Chapter 4).

Rent-seeking

In Buchanan's analysis the exploitative potential of democracy is inextricably linked to the idea of rent-seeking. The notion of rent-seeking as used in academic political economy was first developed by Gordon Tullock (1967), although the specific term 'rent-seeking' was originally coined by Anne Krueger (1974). Rent-seeking pertains to the actions of profit-seeking individuals in economic and political contexts.

In economic theory (as opposed to everyday language), a rent describes a payment made to the owner of a resource over and above what that resource could command in an alternative usage. As Buchanan has put it: 'So long as owners of resources prefer more to less, they are likely to be engaged in rent seeking, which is simply another word for profit seeking' (LFCL, p. 103).

In an economic context, rent-seeking may lead, for example, the sole baker in a remote village to charge the price for bread that maximizes his or her profits. In the short-term, the baker may be able to reap exceptional returns if there is no convenient alternative source of bread. In the long-term, however, the existence of these exceptional profits may motivate other producers to establish competing bakeries, or inspire consumers to source alternative suppliers of bread. In the marketplace, then, rent-seeking has socially beneficial consequences because it acts as a spur to entrepreneurial activity that eventually erodes and dissipates those rents. The overall consequence of the process is increased efficiency as resources are allocated to more productive uses as signalled by the profit-seeking activities of economic rent-seekers (LFCL, pp. 103–107).

In the political realm, however, rent-seeking tends to have socially pernicious consequences. Political rents do not exist 'naturally', but are deliberately created by those with political authority, usually via the allocation of a monopoly right or special privilege to a particular individual or group. Political rent-seeking involves the attempt to persuade the government to create or allocate such rents. For example, a telecoms company may seek the monopoly right to create a mobile telephone network; a car manufacturer may try to persuade the government to ban foreign imports; or milk producers may lobby for government subsidies to protect their profits. In contrast to economic rents, once a monopoly right or special privilege has been granted by political authority it will tend to be exploited repeatedly, with little prospect of erosion or dissipation (LFCL, pp. 108–112).

The allocation of political rents involves a transfer of resources from one group to another, such as from consumers to producers, or from one group of producers to another. In this sense, political rent-seeking is another example of exploitation via the political process described in the preceding section – a process via which 'the winners secure differential payoffs; the losers are exploited' (PPNI, p. 45; See also CoC, Chapter 19).

Following Tullock's (1967) ground-breaking analysis of the welfare implications of political rent-seeking, Buchanan has argued that political rent-seeking not only reduces the welfare of particular individuals, but also imposes welfare losses on the economy as a whole. Rent-seeking imposes costs on the whole economy because scarce resources will be devoted to rent-seeking activity and not allocated to alternative, more productive, uses; resources that would otherwise be invested in economic production will be devoted to political campaigning and lobbying. Similarly, skilled and talented individuals will use their abilities in political entrepreneurialism rather than engaging in wealth-creating economic innovation. Political rent-seeking therefore imposes opportunity costs on society as a whole, even upon those individuals and groups who ostensibly gain from rent-seeking. According to Buchanan, 'attempts will be made to capture these [political] rents, and resources used up in such attempts will reflect social waste, even if the investments are fully rational for all participants' (LFCL, p. 109; See also: RoR, pp. 131–135).

Buchanan has argued that the resources lost to rent-seeking activity will be directly related to the size and scope of government intervention in the economy. The larger the size of the public sector and the greater the level of government regulation of economic activity, the greater will be the opportunities for people to engage in political rent-seeking and the potential rents to be gained. Hence, the welfare losses resulting from rent-seeking are inextricably linked to the size of the state (LFCL, pp. 108–111).

Although political rents may be very difficult to remove once established, the precise beneficiaries of those rents may change as members of the losing minority attempt to attain membership of the winning coalition. This leads to the 'majority cycle': the cyclical creation of new majority coalitions that aim to exploit the potential gains from rent-seeking in a given polity. The existence of the 'majority cycle' means that no one can be absolutely certain of being in the winning (exploiting) coalition in the future; everyone faces the possibility of being a member of the losing (exploited) group. As a consequence, individuals may be reluctant to invest in wealth creation, even when they are members of the winning coalition, because of the constant risk of exile to the exploited group and the resultant confiscation of the wealth that has been created. Indeed, successful wealth creation is likely to lead to expulsion from the majority coalition as others organize to capture that wealth. It is argued that if there is a risk that profits may be transferred to others via the political process at some point in the future, people will not invest in wealth-creating activities. Consequently, political rent-seeking is said to lead to the relative impoverishment of society as a whole (RoR, pp. 131–135).

According to Buchanan, then, rent-seeking exists in both economic and political processes. However, the consequences of rent-seeking are markedly different in the two institutional settings. In the marketplace: 'The unintended results of competitive attempts to capture monopoly rents are "good" because entry is possible'. In the political realm, by contrast, 'comparable attempts to capture artificially contrived advantageous positions under governmentally enforced monopoly are "bad" because entry is not possible' (LFCL, p. 108).

Hence, rent-seeking in the economic realm tends to draw in new entrants that erode and dissipate the exceptional profits of a monopoly position, leading to welfare gains, whereas political rent-seeking tends to involve the exclusive allocation of monopoly rights that grant and/or entrench exceptional profits, leading to welfare losses. Even if control of the monopoly right may be cyclical, the overall welfare losses it entails will be constant. In this way, the expansion of the state into productive activities beyond its simple protective role tends to produce outcomes contrary to the interests of the individuals who initially wish to extend the political realm to the supply of public goods.

The state: the threat of Leviathan

In Buchanan's account of the social contract, individuals voluntarily agree to surrender some of their freedom to an over-arching political authority in order to escape the problems of anarchy. By so doing, those individuals also create a new institutional dimension: the state. The creation of the state may initiate a whole host of new troubles, problems and dilemmas. These difficulties were recognized in the title of Hobbes's (1651) classic account of the social contract: *Leviathan*, the name Hobbes gave to his envisaged post-contract commonwealth, was also the name of a biblical sea monster that lurked in the depths of the ocean ready to drag unwitting mariners to their doom.

Brennan and Buchanan (RoR, pp. 128–129) have noted that many accounts of politics entirely neglect the existence of the state. For example, many accounts of distributive justice involve the division of a wealth pie between different people; the salient question is assumed to be how the pie is to be distributed between the various claimants. Such a question, however, assumes an additional actor. In addition to the claimants to the aggregate pie, there is now also the person who will cut the pie and allocate the different shares. Indeed, framing the question in terms of how the pie is to be divided and distributed gives ownership of the pie to the cutter/allocator. Therefore, an important question arises: how much of the pie will the cutter/allocator keep for his or her personal consumption?

If those who control the state are selfless or benign, then this question may be moot. But in reality, as Buchanan has described throughout his work, the state may be controlled by a despot committed to appropriating the pie for personal consumption, or allocating large portions of the pie to the people he or she happens to favour. That 'despot' need not be a Caligula-type figure, but may be a democratic majority or its representatives.

The state poses a particularly grave threat to individual liberty because of the extraordinary role that it is required to perform and the extraordinary power that is invested in it. The role of the state as the one lawful protection and enforcement agency with a monopoly on the legitimate use of violence within its territory means that the potential for tyranny and abuse of power by those who control the state may be very great. The problem then becomes, in the words of the Roman poet Juvenal, *Quis custodiet ipsos custodes?* That is, who will guard the guardians? The theoretical agreement of a social contract that establishes an enforcement agency thereby creates the problem that: 'There is no obvious and effective means through which the enforcing institution or agent can itself be constrained in its own behavior' (LoL, p. 87).

The problem of controlling the state is at the centre of Buchanan's analysis of the pathologies of politics and is bound up with the belief that the dynamics of the modern state lead it to inexorably expand. Buchanan's work provides an account of how the incentives faced by the three principal categories of political actors – voters, politicians and bureaucrats – may all lead to the growth of the state.

First, as described in detail above, Buchanan has shown that democratic voting procedures are a flawed mechanism for translating individual preferences into public policies that lead to the over-supply of most public goods and services and the consequent expansion of the size and scope of the state. In particular, the fact that political choices are often uncosted, frequently bundled together, and the distribution of benefits and burdens may be uncertain, means that when people choose collectively via voting they are likely to choose more than they would when choosing as private individuals (e.g. LFCL, pp. 75–88; CoC, particularly Chapter 14; PFDP, particularly Chapters 2 and 6; LoL, particularly Chapter 9).

The ability of majority and minority coalitions to impose costs on others set out above may also drive the growth of the state. Where voters are able to assign themselves benefits that are paid for by others they are likely to vote for policies and programmes that they would not choose if they personally had to bear the full costs. For this reason, the exploitative potential of majoritarian democracy is likely to lead to an increase in the size and scope of government above what would be chosen if individual taxpayers-voters paid the full cost of personal benefits received.

The logic of Buchanan's analysis leads to the conclusion that the vagaries of the political process lead to the expansion of the state beyond what people would rationally choose when agreeing to the social contract. People do not intend to create Leviathan, but Leviathan emerges from the way that choices are framed in a political context. Similarly expansionary consequences follow from the incentives faced by politicians.

In *The Limits of Liberty*, Buchanan argued that politicians seek 'political income' from elected office. This 'income' may not necessarily be monetary. Rather, politicians fall into three broad categories: ideologues who wish to pursue a specific policy agenda; opportunists who are not particularly driven but nevertheless enjoy the prestige and status that comes from elected office; and finally those who seek pecuniary gains from political office (LoL, pp. 197–201).

Ideologues who achieve elected office are likely to expand the role of government simply because those who aim to utilize the political process to achieve positive social ends are more likely to be socialist believers in big government than their small government counterparts:

[T]hose persons who place relatively high values on the ability to influence collective outcomes, and who do so in the genuinely incorruptible sense of desiring to 'do good' for the whole community, are quite likely to be those who seek to accomplish their own preferred social objectives through collective or governmental means. By contrast, those persons who, ideologically, desire that the governmental role in society should be reduced to minimal levels are unlikely to be attracted to politics. Few natural anarchists or libertarians frequent capital [i.e. government] cloakrooms. (LoL, p. 199)

Buchanan argued, then, that idealists who enter politics with 'pure' motives are more likely to favour policies that expand the state than policies that reduce the role of government.

But not all politicians are ideologically motivated. Many politicians may have ill-defined policy objectives and may be attracted to elected office out of a vague commitment to public service, or 'because they enjoy positions of leadership and authority, positions that make it necessary for other persons actively to seek them out and solicit their assistance' (LoL, p. 199).[10] The instrumental goal of such politicians may be to help as many people as possible, or more simply to obtain and retain elected office. Achieving either goal will mean satisfying the preferences of as many voters as possible, which is likely to place expansionary pressure on the public budget:

> The politician who secures his utility only because he chooses for and thereby pleases the largest number of constituents will find that favorable action on differentially beneficial spending projects offers more reward than favorable action reducing general tax-costs . . . because the benefits from government spending may be differentially directed toward particular subgroups in the community, politicians are motivated to initiate the formation of coalitions that will exploit these latent demand opportunities. (LoL, p. 200)

A non-ideological politician, then, with no prior commitment to increasing the size of the state, will nevertheless encounter powerful incentives to build voting coalitions that result in an expansion of the role and activities of government.

A third category of politician considered by Buchanan is those who seek pecuniary gain from elected office. Buchanan argued that the actions of these politicians will similarly expand the public budget because their ends are more likely to be satisfied by an increase in the role of government than by a reduction in the size of the state:

> With minimal governmental intrusion into the economy, with minimal and quasi-permanent spending

components, the grasping politician may have little or no opportunities for graft. However, with a complex public sector, and one that involves new and expanding spending programs, there may be numerous opportunities. In a newly enacted program, one without established guidelines and procedures, politicians may find ample sources for direct and indirect kickbacks from the producers and producing firms whose rents are enhanced by the program. Such officials will, therefore, seek continually to enlarge budgets and, especially, to introduce new and different programs. (LoL, p. 200)

A corrupt politician, then, will find that his or her venality is best served by the expansion of the state, whereas a diminution in the role of government is likely to reduce the opportunities for pecuniary acquisition.

Buchanan argued, then, that whether politicians are ideologues, opportunists or profiteers, 'each will be motivated to expand the size and scope of the governmental sector of the economy' (LoL, p. 201).

A second category of state actor, in addition to politicians, is government employees, or bureaucrats. Buchanan has argued that, like individual voters and politicians, bureaucrats encounter incentives that lead them to support expansion of the size and scope of the state.

According to Buchanan, it is logical that government employees, like the employees of private enterprises, will want to see their organizations expand. A growing organization (as opposed to one that is shrinking) offers greater job security and better prospects of promotion and/or salary increases: '[A bureaucrat] knows that his career prospects, his chances for promotion and tenure in employment, are enhanced if the size of the distinct budgetary component with which he is associated increases' (LoL, p. 204).

A government official, therefore, will 'exercise his own choices, whenever possible, to increase rather than to decrease project and agency budgets' (LoL, p. 204). The bureaucrat, however, chooses as both a voter and a government employee. The unique dynamic of the modern democratic state is that public sector workers have full voting rights and enjoy government salaries and working conditions that are determined via the political process rather than in competitive markets. As a result, 'the prospective or actual [government] employee becomes a built-in supporter of budgetary expansion and a built-in opponent of budgetary reduction' (LoL, p. 203). When government is a relatively small part of the economy this may be of little significance, but when the public sector employs between a quarter and a half of the total workforce – as is the case in most contemporary democracies – then government employees (and prospective government employees) and their dependents become a significant voting bloc that may be inherently hostile to reducing the size of the government and inherently supportive of increasing it.

Not only can government officials be expected to vote for parties and policies that would expand the public budget, Buchanan argued that their actions as employees can be expected to support government growth. Legislative decisions are likely to leave substantial scope for bureaucratic discretion and this scope is likely to be exercised in favour of budgetary expansion:

> There is little or no potential reward to the governmental employee who proposes to reduce or limit his own agency or bureau. Institutionally, the individual bureaucrat is motivated toward aggrandizement of his own agency.

And, since the effective alternatives for most governmental employees are other agencies and projects, this motivation for expansion will extend to government generally. (LoL, p. 204)

Government employees, like voters and politicians, face incentives that lead them to support the expansion of the state. As more and more people are employed by the government, a dynamic of more and more government growth may develop. Again, this will mean that over time the state will grow beyond what was envisaged by the individuals who originally entered into the social contract.

Buchanan's analysis, then, shows that the choices people make in the political realm produce an internal dynamic that drives the growth of the state. The cumulative impact of the actions of individuals in the political realm is to expand the state far beyond what is reasonably likely to be agreed in any hypothetical social contract.

The consequence, according to Buchanan, is that people unwittingly create a vast and complex bureaucratic structure whose actions seem beyond the control of any single individual, so that: 'Man finds himself locked into an impersonal bureaucratic network that he acknowledges to be of his own making' (LoL, p. 188).

A crucial difference between the modern Leviathan of majoritarian democracy and the monarchical autocracies of the past, however, is that the modern Leviathan is staffed and controlled by people fundamentally identical to those who do not wield power:

> Modern man cannot place himself in opposition to a government that is staffed and directed by an exterior elite, by members of a wholly different order or estate.

To an American patriot, there was George III. To a member of the French bourgeoisie, there was the ancien régime. To the followers of Lenin, there was the Russian aristocracy. To modern man tangled in the web of bureaucracy, there is only himself, or others of his same breed. (LoL, p. 188)

The modern state, then, is not controlled by a distinct elite or a unique political class. Although those who attain high political office may share particular personality characteristics, those who govern and those who are governed nevertheless share the same basic sociological background. There is, for example, little sociological difference between senior lawyers, doctors and academics, and senior governmental actors. Indeed, where between a quarter and a half of the workforce are state employees, a sharp divide between governors and governed must be implausible.

This does not mean, Buchanan stressed, 'that all persons possess equal power of influencing governmental policy in the modern world' (LoL, p. 188). Rather, the point is that the modern Leviathan is a monster that has been created in our own image, so that, 'When we speak of controlling Leviathan we should be referring to controlling self-government, not some instrument manipulated by the decisions of others than ourselves' (LoL, p. 188).

Buchanan identified two principal problems that arise as a result of the growth of government. First, as noted above, the more goods and services are supplied as public goods in the political realm, the more individuals will be required to 'purchase' goods and services at quantities incongruent with their own preferences. Hence, where government accounts for close to half of all economic activity, it is to be anticipated that a majority of the population will fund a bundle of politically supplied goods and services that differs markedly from the bundle they would purchase in private markets. From Buchanan's individualist-democratic perspective, and, indeed, from the perspective of any notion of democracy with popular sovereignty at its centre, this must be considered unsatisfactory. The growth of government, then, distorts the idea that democracy is a mechanism via which people overcome free-rider problems in the supply of goods and services and instead transforms democracy into a setting where the vast majority of people are required to pay for goods and services that they would not to choose to consume in an economic context.

Second, as also noted above, in order to ensure the political supply of such a wide range of goods and services, the productive state is likely to require the assistance of the protective state. Hence, the state apparatus that was initially created to defend property rights will come to be called upon to enforce transfers that effectively infringe property rights. In this way, individuals who may be hypothesized to have created the state to escape the chaos of anarchy where their property rights were constantly violated find themselves returned to a similarly anarchical situation where their property rights are constantly breached by a state over which they seem to have no power or control (LoL, Chapter 6).

A legitimately created state, then, may not stay within the limits that were agreed by the initial contracting parties. Although the formal democratic and legislative processes may enable government to give its actions the trappings of legitimacy, according to Buchanan this does not alter the fact that violations of individual rights by the democratic state are indeed violations. As Brennan and Buchanan described:

> Once established as sovereign, government may not willingly remain within the limits of its initially delegated authority. To the extent that it exceeds these limits, however, government becomes illegitimate in its actions, even in the gloomiest of the Hobbesian visions of contract. Government may, in this setting, take on itself the role of redefining individual rights, but it does so in explicit violation of its contractually legitimate origins. (RoR, p. 31)

Buchanan's analysis of the pathologies of majoritarian democracy suggests that people who contract into the state to escape from the misery of anarchy may find themselves in what Buchanan termed 'constitutional anarchy': a situation where it is government, rather than the absence of an overarching authority, that is the root cause of systematic rights-violation.

This section has set out Buchanan's account of the pathologies of contemporary democratic practice. In particular, it has shown that in a contemporary democracy there will be frequent disparities between individual preferences and the choices that emerge from democratic decision-making processes, meaning that people will be frequently required to pay for goods and services that they do not wish to consume; majorities, and sometimes minorities, will be able to impose external costs on individuals and disorganized segments of the population; political rent-seeking may become endemic; and the creation of the state may invest monopoly power in a single institution that is likely to grow beyond what was envisaged by the individuals who initially agreed to its creation. The following section will present the solutions that Buchanan has proposed to these problems of democratic governance.

Constitutionalism: Solving the Problems of Politics

Buchanan's work provides an account of the problems of anarchy that lead people to enter into the social contract to escape the threat of violent predation in the absence of the protective state. In the political realm, however, the pathologies of majoritarian democracy effectively return people to an anarchical situation where they again face the constant threat of rights-violation by those who control the state. It would appear that people are trapped in a vicious circle where life is intolerable with and without the state. But Buchanan has proposed solutions to the problems of politics.

The most obvious solution to the problems of politics is to keep the politicized realm of society as small as possible. As Buchanan has written in the context of the potential for exploitation inherent to politics: 'any increase in the relative size of the politicized sector of the economy must carry with it an increase in the potential for exploitation' (FLL, p. 68). If goods and services *can* be provided via private markets, then goods and services *should* be provided by private markets so as to avoid the pathologies of the political process set out in the previous section. Political intervention in the economy should be seen as a last resort when and where genuinely insurmountable collective action problems exist.

But given that, as described earlier, the state is a necessary evil because anarchy is not possible, the question that remains is: how are the necessary activities of the state to be undertaken without people's liberties being infringed and without the state expanding to subsume an ever-greater share of economic activity?

Buchanan's answer to this question is founded upon the principle of constitutionalism: the notion that government can only be constrained by the agreement of constitutional rules that set binding limits to what government can do. According to Buchanan, it must now be accepted that the democratic process itself is an insufficient check on the power of government, so constitutional rules that constrain the democratic process are required to keep government within the boundaries that would be agreed in a social contract (LFCL, pp. 51–52; PT, pp. 8–9; CCC, p. 229).

For Buchanan, of course, a constitution describes a set of rules that has unanimous consent and therefore cannot be amended without the unanimous agreement of all the contracting parties. A constitution might be considered analogous to the rules of the game in a sporting contest; it is in the constitutional context that people should seek to control government by setting clear boundaries to what the state may do vis-à-vis individual members of society:

> Constitutional politics involves setting the rules, selecting the parametric framework within which ordinary political decisions are to be made and carried out . . . Such constitutional limits may lay out protected spheres for personal liberties, as in bills of rights, and also economic liberties. (CCC, p. 229)

Normal, day-to-day politics, then, will be 'politics within rules'; political activity will take place within clear, unanimously agreed, constitutional boundaries. Such constitutional rules may develop over time via an evolutionary process, or may be deliberately designed in a constitutional moment. Equally, constitutional rules may be formal or informal. If there is a consensus that government must respect the freedom of the press within a particular society, for example, then even without a formal statutory guarantee of press freedom, freedom of the press may be said to be part of that polity's constitution. The corollary of this point, of course, is that if formal constitution rules are not respected then they are effectively worthless, as has been demonstrated by the written constitutions that have failed to prevent infringements of basic rights, such as the constitution of the German Weimar Republic. The crucial characteristic of a constitution, then, is that it must be quasi-permanent, a set of 'relatively absolute absolutes' upon which there is general agreement (CCC, pp. 229–230).

Constitutional change, just like changes to the sporting rules of the game, alters what is permissible in the post-constitutional setting, or on the field of play. If government is infringing the rights of its citizens, then those citizens must look to the constitutional context to change the relevant rules to better constrain the actions of the state.

Buchanan has proposed three basic ways in which constitutional rules may be used to limit the power of government that will be considered in this section. First and foremost, a 'fiscal constitution' may be enacted to set limits to the power of government in terms of its ability to tax its citizens. Second, simple majority voting rules may be replaced with qualified majority voting procedures. Third, federalism may be a way of limiting the power of the central state. Finally, this section will also consider Buchanan's proposal for a 'constitutional revolution' in contemporary democracies to redraw the social contract to bring about a new constitutional settlement that effectively constrains the power of government.

A fiscal constitution

The power to tax is one of the most significant powers of government. Indeed, Brennan and Buchanan have noted that, 'For the ordinary citizen . . . the power to tax is the most familiar manifestation of the government's coercive power' that 'involves the power to impose, on individuals and private institutions more generally, charges that can be met only by a transfer to government of economic resources' (PT, p. 11). Indeed, all government power follows from its taxing power; if government was unable to appropriate economic resources then no other coercive or intrusive actions would be possible, as the state would be without the means to enforce its will. Constraining the power to tax, then, may be the key to constraining the power of government as a whole.

Buchanan has proposed the introduction of a fiscal constitution to govern the tax-raising powers of the state as a solution to the abuse of the power to tax as a means of extracting resources for purposes not supported by (a majority or a minority of) taxpayers.

The first component of a fiscal constitution would be recognition that tax rules and institutions should be treated as permanent, or quasi-permanent, features of the political system. If tax rules and institutions are not considered part of the meta-framework of politics, then the possibility of exploitation via the political process becomes ever present:

> [If] the allocation of tax shares among individuals and groups in the economy and the choice of tax instruments that generate the imputations of such shares are considered 'up for grabs' during each and every new budgetary period . . . [then] the prospective taxpayer is, of course,

vulnerable to exploitation by government to the maximum limits of his taxpaying capacity. (PT, p. 221)

By moving tax policy into the constitutional realm, the appropriate rules and institutions of taxation, and changes to those rules and institutions, require the unanimous agreement of all the individuals liable to taxation. The potential for exploitation via the political process is then dramatically reduced.

For Buchanan, any plausible account of the agreement of a constitutional contract must involve the agreement of a fiscal constitution. It would be inconceivable that contracting individuals would not wish to agree tax rules and institutions at the constitutional level because failure to do so would leave all parties exposed to the threat of exploitation via future tax policies. Furthermore, the possibility that tax rules and institutions may be subject to radical change at any point in the future would create high levels of uncertainty that may frustrate and inhibit much purposeful planning on the part of both individuals and firms (PT, Chapter 10).

Brennan and Buchanan (PT, Chapter 10) have argued that a fiscal constitution should provide *absolute* and *relative* guarantees for fiscal policy. Absolute guarantees concern the total size of the tax burden irrespective of its division among individual taxpayers. Relative guarantees concern tax arrangements between individuals: how the tax burden is divided between different taxpayers.

An absolute fiscal guarantee *limits the rate of taxation government can levy against a particular source of income or wealth.* Article 13 of the Californian constitution is an example of such an absolute fiscal guarantee. This article prohibits the Californian state from taxing property to more than

1 per cent of its market value and was passed by a two-thirds majority of the Californian population in a state-wide referendum in June 1978. This constitutional amendment was one of a number of 'taxpayer revolts' in the USA in the 1970s and 1980s that imposed constitutional constraints on the ability of state authorities to levy taxation (PT, pp. 229–231).

A constitutional limit on any one source of taxation must limit the total tax take available to government given that income and wealth are derived from multiple sources. As Brennan and Buchanan put it, 'any limit on one tax from among the allowable set available to government must reduce the total revenue potential collectable by government from the whole set' (PT, p. 229). However, a single limit on one source of tax revenue is unlikely to prove an effective constraint on public expenditure in the absence of other constitutional constraints on government action given that there are so many possible sources of tax revenue. Indeed, this point as can be demonstrated by the Californian example where, despite the existence of Article 13, public expenditure increased by 180 per cent between 1990 and 2009 (Summers, 2009).

A second absolute fiscal guarantee is to *limit the tax base* – that is, to limit the sources of income and wealth that can be taxed. Without limits to the tax base all sources of income and wealth are liable to taxation and public expenditure may expand exponentially via a series of seemingly insignificant taxes on many different sources of income and wealth. Brennan and Buchanan (PT, p. 232) have argued that limits to the tax base involve the effective creation of constitutional tax loopholes; an individual may be constitutionally allowed to transfer income or wealth into a particular source, such as property, in order to limit their personal tax burden.

According to Brennan and Buchanan it is logical to suppose 'that the individual at the constitutional stage will seek deliberately to build certain "loopholes" or "escape routes" into the tax structure' (PT, p. 232). In constitutional choice, then, it is argued that choosing individuals will rationally seek to limit the tax base in order to allow those who believe themselves subject to punitive taxation to escape from such demands.

A third absolute fiscal guarantee discussed by Brennan and Buchanan is the *constitutional requirement that government produces a balanced budget* – 'that government cover its outlays with tax revenues rather than with public-debt issue or with new money creation' (PT, p. 236). Brennan and Buchanan argue that prior to the acceptance of Keynesian ideas among policymakers such a requirement was one of the informal rules observed by government actors, but, 'The effect of the Keynesian revolution was to repeal this part of the fiscal constitution' (PT, p. 236).

The constitutional prohibition of public-debt creation may be understood as a further means of limiting the tax base by preventing government from effectively taxing future taxpayers, many of whom will be unable to exercise any form of political control over the budgetary process as they will not yet have been enfranchised. Again, it is argued that in a constitutional moment choosing individuals will rationally wish to introduce such a measure in order to prevent government continually seeking recourse to public debt creation as a means of funding unconstrained spending which will ultimately prove economically ruinous (PT, p. 236).

A fourth absolute fiscal guarantee proposed by Buchanan is the introduction of *earmarked taxation*. Earmarked taxation describes 'the practice of designating or dedicating specific [tax] revenues to the financing of specific public services' (DT, p. 72). In an earmarked system taxpayers receive specific bills for specific services, such as fire protection, policing or highway maintenance, which enables them to identify the cost of each separate good or service. Buchanan has argued that earmarked taxation gives collective decision-making some of the characteristics of individual choice in private markets and thereby ameliorates some of the pathologies of political decision-making that were set out earlier in this chapter (DT, p. 73; PFDP, Chapter 6).

By providing taxpayers-voters with more transparent information about the costs of publicly provided goods and services than would be available if those goods and services were funded from general taxation, earmarked taxation removes some of the uncertainty frequently present in collective choices; earmarked taxation enables individuals to make a more informed evaluation of the costs and benefits of different goods and services than if those goods and services were offered only as component parts of large bundles of potential public services that may constitute a significant proportion of a country's GDP.

According to Buchanan, earmarked taxation enables an individual to ' "vote" independently on the funds to be devoted to schools, to sanitation, and so on, given the specified revenue sources'. So that, '[o]nly in this manner can he make "private" choices on the basis of some reasonably accurate comparison of the costs and benefits of the specific public services, one at a time' (DT, p. 73).

Brennan and Buchanan have argued that an additional benefit of earmarked taxation is that it may restrain the ability of government actors to appropriate public funds. Here, Brennan and Buchanan (PT, p. 179) begin from the assumption that in the real world, as opposed to the idealized models of public finance textbooks, 'fiscal decisions are made by revenue-maximizing politicians-bureaucrats who may have at least some power to secure a share of tax revenues as surplus for themselves'. As described above, if the state is not neutral, but composed of actors with interests of their own, we may reasonably assume that government actors will endeavour to appropriate a share of public funds, for example in the form of increased wages or similar benefits. The ability of politicians-bureaucrats to capture public funds may be limited if such revenues are strictly allocated to the provision of specific goods and services. According to Brennan and Buchanan:

> Effectively designed earmarking may limit the extent to which government, any government, can exploit the taxpaying public; government may be given a positive incentive to provide the goods and services that taxpayers want. The decision makers, whoever these may be, can be kept 'honest'. (PT, p. 180)

Earmarked taxation is logically compatible with both big and small government; it could be argued that earmarking leads to an increase in overall public spending because people will wish to maximize their consumption of individually presented goods and services, whereas choosing at more general levels of public expenditure does not incentivize such profligacy. The more plausible position, however, would seem to be that earmarking leads to an overall reduction in public spending as people do not have to vote for an overall increase in the public budget in order to receive (what they consider to be) optimal levels of supply of those goods and services that they value most highly (DT, pp. 71–88; PFDP, Chapter 6).

Irrespective of the relationship between earmarked taxation and overall levels of public expenditure, Buchanan has argued that a constitutional requirement that all taxation be earmarked offers a way in which public choices made in the political realm can be made more like private choices made in an economic context and the actions of elite political actors may be constrained. As such, Buchanan has argued that earmarked taxation should logically form part of any fiscal constitution designed to limit the pathologies of majoritarian democracy (PT, Chapter 7; DT, pp. 71–100).

The implementation of a relative fiscal guarantee involves giving constitutional status to *the generality principle*. The generality principle describes the idea that government legislation should apply equally to all people: legislation should not apply only to particular individuals, groups, classes, occupations or interests, but should be generally applicable. In contemporary democracies it is generally accepted that it is illegitimate for legislation to discriminate between the sexes and between different racial, religious or ethnic groups, but it is also generally accepted that government may discriminate on the basis of income, wealth, occupation and geographic location, for example when differential tax rates are imposed on different incomes, when special privileges are assigned to particular occupations, or when benefits are allocated to specific localities. The generality principle challenges the belief that such discriminatory legislation is compatible with constitutional democracy.

In Buchanan's account of the social contract it is said to be implausible to believe that people would consent to the creation of a state that was able to use its power to favour particular individuals or groups:

> [B]ecause of each person's interest in the security of his agreed-on rights, the legal or protective state must be characterized by precepts of neutrality. Players would not consciously accept the appointment of a referee who was known to be unfair in his enforcement of the

rules of the game, or at least they could not agree on the same referee in such cases. (LoL, p. 88; See also: PT, pp. 184–190; PPNI, p. 15).

If the notion of the social contract is a meaningful way to establish the legitimacy or otherwise of political institutions and arrangements, then it follows that if discriminatory politics would not be agreed in a contractarian situation then such politics cannot be considered legitimate. Legitimate post- constitutional politics, therefore, must require the application of the generality principle – all legislation must all apply equally to all citizens, regardless of personal, sociological or economic characteristics.

For Buchanan and Congleton, this non-discriminatory politics is 'politics by principle' that may be contrasted with 'politics by interest'. Politics by principle implies that government is constrained by a clear set of constitutional principles, whereas politics by interest describes a government that acts to advance the interests of whatever organized groups have managed to capture the political process or are favoured by elite political actors:

> Politics by principle constrains agents and agencies of government to act nondiscriminatorily, to treat all persons and groups of persons alike, and to refrain from behavior that is, in its nature, selective. Within the limits of such constraints, politics, may do much or little, and it may do what is done in varying ways. (PPNI, p. xx)

Non-discriminatory politics, like earmarked taxation, could conceivably be compatible with both big, interventionist government and small, limited government.

However, non-discriminatory politics does imply that government should act equitably in the allocation of collectively financed benefits and collectively imposed burdens among the individual members of society.

First, this means that, 'A collectively financed and/or supplied good or service, or bundle, must be available to all members of the political unit'. The generality principle is violated if a publicly financed benefit is offered to some members of the polity to the exclusion of others (PPNI, p. 58).

Means-tested benefits, for example, violate the generality principle by assigning a benefit to some people but not others on the basis of income or wealth. Means-tested benefits would appear to offer a Pareto improvement compared to universal benefits via the removal of the deadweight losses of churning in the taxes and benefits system (that is, the cost of collecting taxes and then repaying the same money in benefits), but Buchanan and Congleton have argued that in reality the Pareto improvements seemingly promised by means-tested benefits prove to be a chimera because means-tested benefits incentivize rent-seeking that imposes greater costs than the imagined savings. In particular, where benefits are means-tested, significant resources will be allocated to rent-seeking as different groups compete to be included within the means-tested category. As a result, minorities at the top and bottom of the income distribution may be exploited by people politically mobilizing to extend the boundaries of the means-test to include themselves, and the overall tax burden increases as more and more people qualify for means-tested benefits (PPNI, pp. 163–165).

Second, non-discriminatory politics implies that the allocations of political burdens must not be disproportionally carried by particular individuals or groups. The fact that people differ in their abilities and attributes means that a requirement that people contribute absolutely equally to the provision of public goods and services is unlikely to be chosen by those agreeing to the social contract because a requirement that every individual contributes one fixed sum to the provision of collectively financed goods and services, for example, could result in some people facing an effective marginal tax rate close to 100 per cent. Rather, Buchanan and Congleton have argued that the practical application of the generality principle to the allocation of burdens should be interpreted to imply that the costs of financing publicly provided goods and services should be shared proportionally: 'For example, a tax-sharing scheme satisfies the generality norm when the person who earns $120,000 annually is subject to a tax of $10,000, whereas the person who earns $12,000 annually is taxed for $1,000'. In this case the generality principle, 'requires that each person donate the equivalent of one month's income for financing the jointly shared public good' (PPNI, pp. 60–61).

The generality principle, then, is a constitutional rule that constrains post-constitutional politics by applying the generally accepted principle of equality before the law to politics. The generality principle imposes limits on what the majority can do without undertaking the more difficult task of changing the basic norm of majority rule that governs contemporary democratic politics. Buchanan's advocacy of the principle involves a recognition that majority rule is likely to remain the accepted decision-making rule for the foreseeable future, but seeks to constrain what can be done within the context of majoritarian politics (PPNI, p. 68).

Qualified majority decision-making

For Buchanan, making majoritarian democracy work better is a second-best solution to the introduction of democratic decision-making rules that require more than simple majority support for public policies. Indeed, Buchanan and Congleton wrote that, 'Genuine political reform must accomplish some public reinterpretation of what majoritarian democracy is, along with some practical implementation of such a reinterpretation through explicit constitutional change' (PPNI, p. 20). Hence, substantial amelioration of the pathologies of contemporary politics is thought to require a popular reappraisal of the normative basis and practical functioning of majoritarian democracy, which may be expected to lead to popular support for the use of different (though still democratic) decision-making rules.

As noted earlier in this chapter, one of the central contentions of Buchanan and Tullock's *The Calculus of Consent* was that there is no theoretical, ethical or other logical reason to privilege simple majority rule above all other possible decision-making rules. On the contrary, Buchanan and Tullock argued that there are good reasons for believing that simple majority rule is normatively and practically inferior to other decision-making rules *from a democratic perspective*, given that it allows $(n/2 + 1)$ of the voting population to exploit $(n/2 - 1)$ of their fellows (CoC, p. 82 and also more generally Chapters 7, 10, 11 and 17).

Buchanan and Tullock argued that the solution to many of the pathologies of politics set out in the eighth section of this chapter is the introduction of decision-making rules that would require public expenditure decisions to receive the support of more than $(n/2+1)$ of the voting population (or their representatives) in order to pass into legislation. As noted above, Buchanan and Tullock argued that analysis of the costs and benefits of different decision-making rules logically led to the conclusion that in a moment of constitutional choice people would most probably select different voting rules for different decisions, depending on the nature of the decision being made and the size of the decision-making group (CoC, Part III).

It may be asked, of course, how the prevalence of simply majority rule in real world democratic polities can be reconciled with Buchanan's contention that rational individuals would not select simple majority rule as the principal decision-making rule for post-constitutional choices. The answer, according to Buchanan, is that simple majority rule has been chosen by elite political actors who conceive of politics in non-individualistic terms, rather than being selected by rational individuals in a genuine contractarian agreement (MSMO, pp. 261–264).

Federalism

The problems of politics identified by Buchanan all originate from the monopoly position of the state; the fact that people cannot exit from political decisions in the way that they can exit from market transactions is the root cause of the exploitation that is inherent to relationships in the political realm. The logical solution, then, is to give politics more of the characteristics of markets in terms of people's ability to exit from transactions in which they do not wish to participate. Buchanan has argued that federalism may provide a means of achieving this end (FLL, Parts I and II; PT, Chapter 9).

Federalism involves the assignment of government functions to different levels of governmental organization, normally central, regional and local governments, on the basis of subsidiarity: the principle that matters should be dealt with by the lowest possible level of authority. In a federal polity, then, public goods will be supplied by the lowest possible level of government organization capable of overcoming the collective action problems deemed to thwart private supply.

A federal polity creates the possibility of competition between governmental institutions that may be akin to that found in private markets. As set out by Tiebout (1956) in the classic paper on the subject, if public goods are supplied by a plurality of different local governments and migration between localities is costless, or low cost, then individuals will be able to relocate within the geographical boundaries of the local government unit whose supply of public goods most closely matches their own preferences. Individuals will be able to exit from localities where public good provision does not correspond with their preferences and enter those localities where it does. Such an institutional arrangement, then, provides individuals with an exit option similar to that which exists in private markets and allows the development of a plurality of different models of public goods provision in different localities.

The principle of exit inherent to federalism creates interjurisdictional competition whereby local governments must compete to attract residents-taxpayers. To attract sufficient residents-taxpayers to be financially viable, local authorities must ensure that their tax and spending policies are attractive relative to those of competing authorities. A local authority that was captured by a majority or minority group intent on exploiting others, for example, would logically see the intended exploited group relocate to other authorities, ceteris paribus. Federalism, then, involves weakening the monopoly position of governmental institutions.

The decision by individual residents-taxpayers to stay within a particular authority boundary or to exit may be considered tantamount to the choice people make when agreeing to the original social contract. Although few of the possible contracts/bundles of publically provided goods and services will perfectly reflect any single individual's personal preferences, agreeing to a second-best solution is nevertheless likely to be preferable to life outside the social contract or in the least desirable locality. For this reason, Buchanan has argued that just as we should expect everyone to agree to the social contract, we should also expect everyone to find a local authority that reasonably satisfies their personal preferences. On this basis, federal institutional arrangements may act as a de facto constitutional rule limiting public spending to the level envisaged by the parties to the social contract. As Brennan and Buchanan put it: 'It may be possible that an explicit constitutional decision to decentralize and hence to disperse political authority may effectively substitute for overt fiscal limits' (PT, p. 203).

Constitutional revolution

This chapter has shown the thorough diagnosis of the pathologies of contemporary democratic practice set out in Buchanan's work. At the heart of Buchanan's analysis is the contention that contemporary democracies have moved so far beyond what rational men and women can be reasonably expected to agree to in a constitutional moment that the legitimacy of the modern democratic state must be questioned.

Buchanan has argued that the only long-term solution to the problems of contemporary democracies may be a constitutional revolution – a renegotiation (or perhaps first negotiation) of the social contract that would change the basic rules of the political order to produce a constitutionally constrained state (LoL, Chapters 1 and 10; RoR, Chapter 9).

The radicalism of the proposal and magnitude of the envisaged task have been acknowledged by Brennan and Buchanan:

> We are asking no less than that the basic rules of the socioeconomic-political game be changed, rules that have been in place for decades, and that these changes be made peacefully while the game continues to be played under the old rules. This order is a tall one indeed, and we should be under no delusion that a constitutional revolution will simply emerge, in revolutionary fashion, without a conscious investment of effort. (RoR, p. 167)

Buchanan proposed, then, 'basic, nonincremental changes in the structural order of the community, changes in the complex set of rules that enable men to live with one another, changes that are sufficiently dramatic to warrant the label "revolutionary"' (LoL, p. 212).

Buchanan's constitutional revolution would not, however, involve a group or committee of experts, politicians or bureaucrats devising a new constitution to be presented to or imposed upon the general population. Such an endeavour would conflict with Buchanan's basic individualist-democratic values central to his entire enterprise. Hence, his work does not offer a detailed account of what may emerge from a redrawing of the basic rules governing social intercourse:

> I have not tried to present in detail my own private proposals for constitutional reform; I do not offer a description of the 'good society,' even on my own terms . . . An attempt to describe the social good in detail seems to carry with it an implied willingness to impose this good, independent of observed or prospective agreement

among persons. By contrast, my natural proclivity as an economist is to place ultimate value on process or procedure, and by implication to define as 'good' that which emerges from agreement among free men, independent of intrinsic evaluation of the outcome itself. (LoL, p. 210)

Moreover, the imposition of a new constitutional order on one part of society by another would only replicate the problems of contemporary democracy in which one group imposes its wishes on the rest of society. For Buchanan, 'Little, if any, improvement in the lot of modern man is promised by imposition of new rules by some men on other men' (LoL, p. 213).

Rather, Buchanan has advocated a genuine *contractarian* revolution in which a new set of constitutional rules receives the *unanimous* consent of the population. Such a proposal raises the extremely challenging question of how unanimous consent for a new constitution may be attained. Is it realistically conceivable that people would unanimously agree to a new constitutional settlement in contemporary America, Britain or any other advanced democracy? In particular, would the least economically advantaged citizens of contemporary democracies agree to a social contract that restricted the ability of the state to levy progressive taxation or make financial transfers? In the words of Buchanan: 'how can the rich man (or the libertarian philosopher) expect the poor man to accept any new constitutional order that severely restricts the scope for fiscal transfers among groups?' (LoL, p. 224).

A constitutional revolution would require the consent of both the most and the least advantaged members of society, a level of agreement that may not necessarily be easy to imagine. It may be that some members of contemporary societies may believe they have less to lose from a return to the state of nature than from the agreement of a social contract that places existing property rights on a more secure footing. By raising this question, Buchanan's proposal exposes the arguably tenuous legitimacy of political arrangements in contemporary democracies (and arguably demonstrates the normative and empirical power of the 'mythological' social contract).

Buchanan argued that a solution to this problem may emerge if individuals are willing to renegotiate existing property rights. It may be that a one-off transfer of wealth from the rich to the poor would facilitate mutual agreement of a new constitutional compact:

> The rich man, who may sense the vulnerability of his nominal claims in the existing state of affairs and who may, at the same time, desire that the range of collective or state action be restricted, can potentially agree on a once-and-for-all or quasi-permanent transfer of wealth to the poor man, a transfer made in exchange for the latter's agreement to a genuinely new constitution that will overtly limit governmentally directed fiscal transfers. (LoL, p. 225)

It is possible, according to Buchanan, to conceptualize exchanges of this nature that would be mutually beneficial. Buchanan proposed a simplified two-person example to illustrate his argument. Consider a rich man, A, who nominally owns an asset that yields $100,000 in annual income, which is taxed at 50 per cent, leaving a post-tax income of $50,000. Second, consider a poor man, B, who owns no assets, and earns $5,000 annually from his labour services. The government collects $50,000 in taxes exclusively from the rich man. The benefits from the projects that these taxes fund accrue in such a manner as to provide the rich man with a benefit value of $10,000, and the poor man with a benefit value of $20,000. Suppose that in a new constitutional moment, the rich man offers to transfer to the poor man one-third of his asset that produces a gross income of $33,333 in exchange for the latter's agreement to reduce the size of the governmental budget to zero. The rich man, under this arrangement, retains a new real income of $66,667, higher than under the previous arrangement ($60,000). The poor man, B, secures a real income of $38,333, higher than he secured under the other arrangement ($25,000). Both parties, then, are made better off under the postulated terms of the new contract and it should therefore be possible to at least conceptualize that the unanimous agreement of a social contract could be reached on a similar basis via a series of bilateral negotiations (LoL, p. 225).

Indeed, Buchanan argued that if the rich feared even more punitive taxation in the future, or both rich and poor feared a non-constitutional revolution during which all property rights would be challenged and potentially reassigned, then there may be strong incentives for all to agree a new constitutional contract (LoL, pp. 225–226).

Buchanan's view that property rights may be renegotiated in this way follows logically from his rejection of natural rights in favour of the view that rights exist only so far as they are recognized and respected by individual men and women, as described in the fourth section of this chapter.

Buchanan, then, does not advocate a top-down reassignment of property rights by government. On the contrary, Buchanan proposes a new social contract as a means of escaping from a situation in which property rights are subject to continual reassignment and hence infringement by government. Buchanan does argue, however, that at present laissez-faire cannot be considered a principle of social organization that would command widespread popular support because it is 'too closely associated with the rights of property in the historically determined status quo' (LoL, p. 227). Buchanan argues, then, that a one-off reassignment of property rights is probably a prerequisite of the agreement of a social contract that made possible the creation of a more limited government.

Buchanan also argued that a necessary part of such a process is likely to be the creation of property rights where none previously existed. According to Buchanan, many of the apparent failures of markets and governments, for example in the areas of traffic congestion, pollution and environmental quality, arise from the absence of clearly defined property rights in these areas. For example, it may be argued that problems of pollution are unresolved where the relevant property rights are not clearly defined, meaning that legal remedies of the kind famously envisaged by Coase (1960) are unrealizable. The journey from the present constitutional anarchy to a genuine constitutional democracy is therefore said to involve 'the *creation* of newly defined rights in areas where none now exist, at least none that can offer a basis for predictability and exchange' (LoL, p. 226).

Buchanan argued, then, that the long-term resolution of the problems of majoritarian democracy is likely to involve the agreement of a new social contract involving a mutually advantageous reassignment of existing property rights as well as the creation of new property rights where none previously existed or where they were ill-defined. Although Buchanan has recognized the undoubtedly significant obstacles to such a resolution, he nevertheless has argued that such an outcome offers hope of achieving the Enlightenment dream of the creation of free societies in which men and women live free from the threatening shadow of an all-powerful state (LoL, pp. 227–228).

Conclusion

This chapter has set out the key components of James Buchanan's intellectual contribution. Buchanan's constitutional political economy begins from the premise that rational individuals would hypothetically decide to leave the state of nature to escape the problems of anarchy. Unfortunately in contemporary politics people encounter problems that effectively return them to an anarchical situation where their basic rights are constantly violated by predatory individuals who gain control of the monopoly power vested in the state. For Buchanan, the route out of this political dilemma is the unanimous agreement of a constitution that imposes effective constraints on the power of the state and guarantees mutually agreed property rights.

Buchanan has written, echoing and seconding Hayek's (1960) famous postscript to *The Constitution of the Liberty*, 'Why I Am Not a Conservative', that he, too, is not a conservative (WITANAC, Chapter 1). Rather, Buchanan has stated that his own political philosophy is best understood within the classical liberal tradition. It is not difficult to see the classical liberal, or perhaps libertarian, elements of Buchanan's thought: Buchanan's work is methodological individualist; Buchanan views individual men and women as rational actors; at the heart of Buchanan's work is the fear of the threat posed to the liberty of the individual by the modern state; and Buchanan believes that it is possible to construct political institutions that will safeguard individual liberty.

There are, however, recognizably conservative elements of Buchanan's thought. In particular, Buchanan's emphasis on the importance of informal rules and conventions in maintaining social order would sit very comfortably with most conservative philosophers. Yet Buchanan does not believe that whatever rules or conventions happen to exist in a particular society should be valued simply because they have stood the test of time and therefore in some way reflect the traditional wisdom or norms of that society. On the contrary, Buchanan has advocated the universality of a particular set of rules and conventions that involve respect for individual liberty and private property. Likewise, Buchanan is agnostic as to the value of different social outcomes: his only concern is that decisions should not be imposed contrary to the ends of individual men and women (WITANAC, Chapter 1).

Buchanan's work, then, most comfortably sits within the classical liberal tradition of James Madison, Adam Smith and F. A. Hayek. In a modern scholarly context Buchanan's work may be most satisfactorily described as libertarian, but to definitively place Buchanan in either the classical liberal or libertarian camp is really a relatively futile exercise in semantics. The value of Buchanan's work lies not in his location in a particular intellectual tradition, but in his analysis of the pathologies and possibilities of democracy.

Notes

[1] It should be noted that in *The Calculus of Consent*, Buchanan and Tullock argue that constitutional agreement requires people to

1. enter the constitutional process as 'equals' in terms of status and therefore 'our analysis of the constitution-making process has little relevance for a society that is characterized by a sharp cleavage of the population into distinguishable social classes or separate racial, religious, or ethnic groupings' (CoC, pp. 80–81). Buchanan clearly revises this view in his later *The Limits of Liberty*; see, for example, the discussion of the emergence of slavery on pages 77–78. The discussion in this section has followed Buchanan's later analysis, rather than the earlier view expressed by Buchanan and Tullock.
2. Rawls's (1971) veil of ignorance described the notion that contracting parties should not possess knowledge of their personal circumstances or preferences that would enable them to tailor the social contract to their own advantage. Rawls's 'original position' thus required participants in contractual deliberation to set aside all knowledge of their own personal circumstances and preferences, so that they were assumed to be ignorant of their place in society, class position, social status, as well as their natural abilities, talents and assets. In such a scenario Rawls assumed that people would not choose institutional arrangements that benefitted specific individuals, groups or classes.
3. Apple's official sales figures. See: http://www.apple.com/pr/library/2007/04/09ipod.html.
4. Covering some 28 pages of small print, Condorcet's proof is far too long to reproduce here, but interested readers are recommended to consult the appendix of Black (1958) for a relatively accessible explanation. For a contemporary discussion and empirical example of Condorcet's paradox, see Kurrild-Klitgaard (2001).
5. Part III of *The Calculus of Consent* contains a highly technical and frequently formal analysis of different decision-making results which readers interested in further exploration of these issues may wish to consult.
6. It is worth noting that Buchanan and Tullock (CoC, pp. 37–38) make the point that in iterated voting situations logrolling or vote-trading may take place that will enable individuals to predict with some accuracy the likely choices of other voters, thereby reducing the more profound problems of uncertainty that would plague a single unique voting event.
7. For ease of comprehension, this model has been adapted slightly from the precise one presented by Buchanan and Tullock

(CoC, pp. 127–128), though the basic characteristics and conclusions remain the same.

8. It is worth noting that in practice this pathology of democracy may be mitigated by the ability of a homogenous, organised minority to capture the political process and impose its views on the majority (as will be discussed in the next sub-section).

9. Indeed, empirical research in the UK has suggested that the middle classes are among the principal beneficiaries of the modern welfare state (Goodin and Le Grand, 1987).

10. This contention is certainly supported by empirical evidence that shows that elected representatives are often not highly motivated or particularly driven, but nevertheless receive important psychic benefits from political office. See, for example, Barber (1965); Meadowcroft (2001); and Rao (1998).

Chapter 3

The Reception and Influence of Buchanan's Work

Introduction

James M. Buchanan has been an extraordinarily influential scholar whose work has made a lasting impact on the disciplines of economics, political economy and political science. It is not difficult to find evidence to support this assertion: first and foremost, Buchanan was awarded the Nobel Prize in recognition of his scholarly contribution; his work has been published in the leading academic journals and by the most prestigious scholarly presses; between 1998 and 2003 his entire output up to that date was collected in twenty volumes by Liberty Fund.

The sub-discipline of public choice theory that Buchanan played a key role in founding has become one of the most important analytical approaches within economics, political economy and political science. Green and Shapiro (1994, p. 3) calculate that in the leading US political science journal, *American Political Science Review*, the proportion of articles utilizing a rational actor model indicative of the public choice approach rose from less than 10 per cent between 1952 and 1967 to close to 40 per cent in the early 1990s.

Even those instinctively hostile to public choice theory have had to concede that it has significant analytical and explanatory power. Dunleavy (1991, p. xi), for example, has written that he began studying public choice solely in order 'to develop an *ad hominem* critique' of the approach, but found that 'ten years later, much of my research has been restructured around a particular kind of institutional public choice method', so that he 'could not pursue research without using [the methodological approach of public choice]'.

As the one of the founders and arguably the most important exponent of public choice theory, Buchanan has been at the forefront of the development and advance of the sub-discipline. This chapter will consider Buchanan's reception and influence in three principal respects. First, the chapter will set out the intellectual impact of public choice theory on the disciplines of political science, economics and political economy in terms of the spread and acceptance of public choice ideas. Second, the chapter will consider the large critical literature generated in response to public choice theory that principally seeks to challenge the basic assumptions of the sub-discipline. Third, the chapter will chart the development of public choice as an academic research community with its own organisations, journals and research centres.

The Intellectual Impact and Influence of Public Choice Theory

In Chapter 1 it was described that when Buchanan began work in the 1950s on his earliest papers, applying the basic analytical framework of mainstream economics to the political realm, such an enterprise had not been undertaken before in a systematic way. It is probably not surprising, then, that while these papers retain a vitality and clarity to this day, for anyone with a basic knowledge of public choice theory much of the content will seem familiar.

Similarly, on its publication in 1962 Buchanan and Tullock's *The Calculus of Consent* was received as a groundbreaking contribution to political economy. Anthony Downs, for example, described it as 'a brilliant and significant contribution to the literature' that 'developed some extremely useful insights' (Downs, 1964, p. 87). But to new readers today the book may appear to be little more than a series of relatively straightforward applications of economic theory to the problems of political decision-making. Buchanan, then, is a scholar whose best-known work has become so influential that some of its novelty and originality may not be immediately apparent to new readers.

In order to bring out Buchanan's scholarly impact, this section will explore three areas in which Buchanan's work has been most influential to the development of scholarship in political economy and to our understanding of political and economic processes.

First and foremost, Buchanan's work has shown that the standard principles of economic analysis can be applied to the political realm to generate insights with real explanatory power. At its core, economics is the study of the actions of rational, self-interested individuals who seek to achieve their ends as consumers and producers in private markets. Buchanan's work transposes the same rational, self-interested individual to a different institutional context: the political realm of politicians, bureaucrats, voters and taxpayers.

As will be discussed in the next section, the application of the principles of economics to politics has proved highly controversial among those who believe that there is a fundamental difference between the political and economic realms and, in particular, that in a political context people can set aside their self-interest to purse the 'common good'.

Nevertheless, a strong claim can be made that the application of behavioural symmetry to economics and politics can foster insights that would not otherwise be forthcoming. For example, in Chapter 2 it was shown that according to Buchanan the presence of uncertainty has very different consequences for an individual attempting to achieve his or her ends via political or via economic processes. In the economic realm an individual's decision to purchase a house, a car or a cup of coffee, for example, will lead him or her to acquire ownership of that good. In the political realm, on the other hand, an individual's decision to choose (i.e. vote for) a particular policy or candidate does not necessarily mean that the policy will be implemented or the candidate will be victorious because the outcome is dependent upon the votes of the other participants in the decision-making process, which cannot be predicted with absolute certainty. The uncertainty present in the political process may lead an individual to seek to second-guess the choices of their fellows and vote for policies or candidates that are not their first preference but that they think have some prospect of electoral success. Hence, the same rational, self-interested individual choosing in the economic and political realms may make very different selections even though their preferences are constant.

Buchanan, then, was a path-breaker, leading the early public choice theorists out of the disciplinary terrain of economics into the terrain of politics. His work showed that the principles of economics could be applied to the political realm to produce new insights that pointed towards viable explanations of why people make very different choices in political and economic contexts; it was not that people's motivations or characters were magically transformed when they entered the political realm, but that these different institutional settings led people of identical character and motivation to make different choices.

The application of economic analysis to politics logically leads to the second of Buchanan's most influential contributions: the insight that the institutional context in which people act will be an important determinant of the choices made therein. A central tenet of public choice theory, then, is that the rules of the game determine the outcomes produced.

At the most basic level, this means that different voting rules will lead to different outcomes even if preferences are constant. As discussed in the previous chapter, in *The Calculus of Consent* Buchanan and Tullock demonstrated this point with the simple example of five people voting to decide on the division of the one and only lot of manna that has fallen from heaven. If the decision is made by a simple majority voting rule, the first three individuals to form a voting coalition will secure control of the manna. But if a voting rule requiring a threshold of two-thirds of the population is introduced, a fourth member of the coalition is required to gain control of the manna. The two different voting rules produce different outcomes in terms of the proportion of the population whose views must be taken into account in dividing the manna: the first rule gives control of the manna to any three people acting in unison, whereas the second rule requires four people to act together to gain control of the resource (CoC, p. 122).

At a more advanced level, it can be shown that the institutional context in which goods and services are provided may determine the quantities that are selected, again holding constant the preferences of the individual choosers. Hence, an individual who would choose x quantity of healthcare in a private market, may choose y quantity in a political context, perhaps because y was the closest to x among the alternative bundles of policies offered by the different political parties, or because y was the least-worst option that the individual thought had a chance of electoral success.

The recognition of the importance of the institutional dimension and the assumption that both economic and political actors are rational and self-interested are interrelated. If individual motivation was assumed to change when people moved between different institutional dimensions, then it would not be possible to isolate and investigate the impact of those different institutions on people's choices. As Brennan and Buchanan put it: 'If . . . different models of human behavior were used in economic (market) and political contexts, there would be no way of isolating the effects of changing the institutions from the effects of changing the behavioral assumptions' (RoR, p. 56). It is the attribution of symmetrical motives to political and economic actors by public choice theorists that has allowed the importance of the institutional dimension to come to the fore.

Buchanan's work may be understood as an important contribution to the development of the new institutional economics in the second half of the twentieth century. This field of research has drawn attention to the importance of institutions in determining outcomes, for example in economic development and in industrial organization. Buchanan's work, of course, has emphasized the importance of the constitutional dimension and the way that the rules of the political game influence the outcomes of the political process.

Buchanan's third most influential contribution has been to consistently highlight the prevalence of government failure and the importance of approaching political economy as an exercise in *comparative* institutional evaluation. Prior to the emergence of public choice theory evidence of market failure was often assumed to logically justify government intervention as a corrective. It was assumed that governments must be able to improve upon market failure, rather like the apocryphal story of the Roman singing contest recounted by Boettke (1998, p. 27):

> According to ancient legend, a Roman Emperor was asked to judge a singing contest between two participants. After hearing the first contestant, the Emperor gave the prize to the second on the assumption that the second could be no worse than the first. Of course, this assumption could have been wrong; the second singer might have been worse. The theory of market failure committed the same mistake as the Emperor.

The theory of market failure, then, committed the mistake of assuming that government intervention could do no worse than the market. Public choice theory showed that in fact government failure could impose far higher costs on the individuals concerned than market failure. According to Boettke (1998, p. 27), 'Many scholars burst the bubble of this romantic vision of the political sector during the 1960s. But it was Buchanan and Gordon Tullock who deserve the credit for shifting scholarly focus'.

Buchanan's work, then, was crucial in ending the dominant romantic view of politics as a process that always produced outcomes that were intended and desired. As set out in the previous chapter, Buchanan's work contains an account of why government failure may be systemic because democratic processes do not accurately translate individual preferences into public policies, the political process may be used as a vehicle for the exploitation of one group by others, politics may be prone to endemic rent-seeking, and because the monopoly power of the state may threaten the liberty of individual citizens.

As a result of the impact of public choice theory it is no longer acceptable for scholars to suppose that evidence of market failure provides a conclusive case for government intervention. Rather, it is now incumbent upon scholars to demonstrate that the outcomes produced by government will improve on those produced by the market in the light of our knowledge of the systemic nature of government failure. Buchanan's work has made an important contribution to the scholarly understanding of political economy as a comparative enterprise.

The Critics of Buchanan and Public Choice Theory

The development and advance of public choice theory has generated a large volume of critical commentary. For many scholars, the application of economic ideas and analysis to the political realm is an unwelcome example of academic imperialism that unsuccessfully conflates two distinct and incompatible scholarly disciplines. Most of the critiques of public choice theory focus on the assumptions that underpin the sub-discipline; it is argued that the conclusions generated by public choice theorists tend to be largely the product of a series of false assumptions about human behaviour and human society.

Methodological individualism

The critiques of public choice theory have largely focused upon the methodological individualism inherent to the public choice approach. As set out in Chapter 2, the key foundational assumption of Buchanan's thought is methodological individualism, the notion that 'Only individuals choose; only individuals act', and therefore, 'An understanding of any social interaction process must be based on an analysis of the choice behavior of persons who participate in the process' (MSMO, p. 56; See also: CCC, pp. 8–9; CoC, Chapter 1; LoL., Chapter 1).

The most basic critique of methodological individualism is that it is a misleading account of the world that wrongly views individuals in isolation from the social context in which they live. According to Petracca (1991, p. 178), 'The problem with methodological individualism is [that it] encourages a political science which empirically views individual actions as unconditioned by social structures and other supra-individual entities'.

Anyone who has read the second chapter of this book will know that this argument does not succeed as a criticism of Buchanan's methodological individualism; at the centre of Buchanan's work is the study of the impact of institutions on individual decisions. Indeed, the essence of constitutional political economy is the study of how different constitutional rules and conventions influence individual choices and outcomes. Hence, the impact of supra-individual entities on individual actions is the central focus of Buchanan's work.

Udehn (1996, Chapter 4) has recognized the importance of institutions to Buchanan's work, but has argued that there is an unresolved and irresolvable tension between Buchanan's methodological individualism and his emphasis on the role of institutions:

> Institutionalism, based on the conviction that institutions matter, implies that institutions have a power of their own. But if they do, we have an explanation of actions in terms of rules, as distinguished from rational choice. Hence, rational choice is not a universal approach in social science. (Udehn, 1996, p. 174)

This argument, however, fails to properly appreciate the relationship between individuals and institutions in Buchanan's work; it does not follow that demonstration of the importance of institutions in some way contradicts or disproves methodological individualism.

For Buchanan, institutions are the product of individual agency; although institutions can be created without human design (language and the market would be examples of this), institutions cannot be created without human action. Of course, individuals may inherit institutions, or have to live with institutions created by others (e.g. when one group imposes rules on another), and in this sense it is possible for individuals to have to live in the context of institutions that they themselves did not create, but this does not change the fact that the existence of institutions should be understood in terms of the choices and actions of individuals. Institutions cannot act; only individuals can act. The law, for example, is undoubtedly an important institution in people's lives, but laws are created, enforced and observed (or not) by individuals – to suggest otherwise is to misunderstand the facts of the world around us.

Buchanan's constitutional political economy involves analysis of individual choice within the context of different political and economic institutions. A central contention of this analysis is that people will make different choices in different institutional settings. Again, this is entirely consistent with methodological individualism: the unit of analysis and the sole actor remain the individual. Hence, as Buchanan has written, 'methodological individualism does not imply or require that individual choice behavior is invariant over changes in the institutional setting, that people choose "as if" they exist in social isolation, one from another' (MSMO, p. 56).

Rather than individualism and institutionalism being the source of a problematic tension in Buchanan's work, it may be more accurate to suggest that Buchanan's unique contribution is founded upon a coherent analysis of the relationship between individuals and institutions via an account of the rational choices of individual men and women in different institutional contexts.

Udehn has also questioned the value-neutrality of Buchanan's methodological individualism. As described in Chapter 2, a central tenet of Buchanan's approach is the rejection of the notion that policies or outcomes can be judged according to a scale of values other than the subjective, personal values held by individual men and women. In Buchanan's early work, at least, it was claimed that such a position was value-neutral as it did not privilege any particular conception of the good life over any other (e.g. CoC, Chapter 1; LoL, Chapter 1). Udehn (1996, pp. 176–184), however, has argued that this position is in fact not value-neutral as Buchanan's claims. Rather, it is said that to argue that the ultimate source of values must be individual men and women is itself a normative and hence value-laden position. According to Udehn, then, Buchanan's individualism is not only methodological, but also ethical, and this is problematic for Buchanan's claim to be engaged in a value-free, scientific exercise rather than a normative, political enterprise.

As Udehn (1996, p. 178) has pointed out, in his later work Buchanan does seem to accept a distinction between two different types of individualism: first, methodological individualism in terms of the study of the rational choices of individual actors, and, second, ethical individualism in terms of the belief that the ultimate source of values should be the values of individual men and women rather than the values preferred by social researchers or some other category of rarefied persons (e.g. CCC, p. 9).

Udehn is clearly correct to suggest that Buchanan's (CCC, p. 9) position that 'locates the ultimate sources of value exclusively in individuals' is not value-free – here Buchanan does advance a normative position. However, it is important to note that Udehn is not suggesting that Buchanan is rejecting a value-free position in favour of a normative one. Instead, what follows from Udehn's criticism is that Buchanan selects one of two normative positions: to locate the sources of value in criteria external to individual men and women, or to locate the sources of value in the values of individual men and women. As such, Udehn's objection does not provide reasons to believe other methodological positions are superior to methodological individualism. Rather, it suggests that – in common with other methodological approaches – methodological individualism involves a normative judgement as to the ultimate source of values.

This section will now examine two aspects of methodological individualism that have attracted widespread criticism: the assumptions of self-interest and rationality on the part of individual actors.

Self-interest

One of the principal assumptions of Buchanan's work, and of public choice theory more generally, is that economic and political actors are fundamentally self-interested. That is, individuals are assumed to conceive of their own ends and to enter the political and economic realms in order to pursue those ends (e.g. CoC, p. 3; PT, p. 19).

The empirical validity of this assumption of symmetrical motivation in the economic and political dimensions has been challenged. Self (1993, p. 6), for example, has argued that 'Altruism appears to be a much more widespread factor in political than in market behaviour'. In particular, it is argued that ideology may be a motivating force in politics, but not in the marketplace, meaning that people are much more likely to pursue other-regarding ends when they enter the political realm than in their market transactions (Self, 1993, pp. 6–7).

This critique, however, appears to add substantive content to the notion of self-interest as utilized by public choice theorists where none is intended to be present. As described in Chapter 2, the assumption of individual self-interest as articulated by Buchanan and others does not imply any substantive content. Individual self-interest may entail a desire to eliminate poverty, protect wildlife or purchase clothes from Prada – the pursuit of each end could fall within an individual's self-interest.

The critique articulated by Self seems to assume that self-interest must be narrowly hedonistic or equivalent to selfishness, when Buchanan and Tullock, for example, explicitly state that, 'The representative individual in our models may be egoist or altruist or any combination thereof' (CoC, p. 3). For Buchanan, an individual who is concerned about the conservation of the environment will act in accordance with this concern in both their economic and political decision-making, and, similarly, an individual whose principal end is to maximize their family's income will act accordingly in both the political and economic contexts.

This basic critique of the self-interest assumption, then, would appear to spring from the mistaken belief that self-interest implies hedonism and/or selfishness when in fact public choice theorists intend only to capture the notion that individuals conceive of their own ends, which may be selfish, altruistic or some combination of the two, and then pursue those ends in their economic and political actions.

A somewhat more sophisticated version of the critique of the self-interest assumption, however, involves the objection that while Buchanan and other public choice theorists may claim that their model of self-interest does not imply any substantive content, this claim is in fact disingenuous because in practice the application of the self-interest assumption always requires that people pursue narrowly hedonistic, self-regarding ends. According to Jeffrey Friedman (1996, p. 22): 'Buchanan and Tullock do, in fact, go on to assume [narrowly hedonistic] self-interested ends, and accordingly they abandon their "praxiological" or thin-rational agnosticism in favor of thick-rational, *Homo economicus* assumptions'.

It is argued that analysis of actual public choice modelling shows that the self-interest assumption has been used to dismiss the whole realm of human behaviour directed towards the achievement of collective or other-regarding ends while simultaneously claiming that all such behaviour may be encapsulated within the self-interest assumption (Petracca, 1991, pp. 178–181).

It is certainly true, as described in Chapter 2, that public choice theorists do reject the notion that there is an objective public interest that can be identified and pursued. Hence, when individuals act in what they think is the public interest, for public choice theorists they are by definition acting in their own self-interest – they are acting on the basis of what *they consider to be* the public interest (e.g. CoC, Chapter 2; LoL, Chapter 6; RoR, Chapter 3). It does not follow, however, that people cannot aspire to act in the public interest. It is simply claimed that an epistemological barrier faces any attempt to do so which means that individuals must in reality pursue their own self-interest.

Public choice theory, then, does require that other-regarding actions are characterized in terms of self-interest. A desire to reduce poverty, for example, may be characterized as an individual's personal preference for less poverty, based on the assumption that other people would prefer to have more income and wealth. Once the desire to reduce poverty is understood as a personal preference representing that individual's self-interest and their personal beliefs about what other people would prefer, then it is perfectly compatible with the foundational assumptions of public choice theory.

Even in the context of the rejection of the existence of an objective public interest, a strong claim can be made that Buchanan and other public choice theorists do not disingenuously attach substantive content to the self-interest assumption. To return to the example used earlier in this chapter adapted from Buchanan and Tullock's *The Calculus of Consent* (p. 122) of five people voting to decide on the division of the one and only lot of manna that has fallen from heaven via two different voting rules, in this example nothing is said about what those individuals will choose to do with the manna from heaven. It may be that all the individuals will be committed egalitarians and therefore will choose to divide the manna equally among the five. Perhaps three of the five wish to distribute the manna among the poor and needy, while the other two wish to retain it for their own consumption. The salient point is that the two different voting rules produce different outcomes in terms of the proportion of the population whose views must be taken into account in dividing the manna. Of course, some of the rhetorical power of the example is derived from the possibility that – depending on the voting rule adopted – three or four of the individuals could divide the manna among themselves to the exclusion of the other(s), but this possibility is not explicitly considered by Buchanan and Tullock. It is left to the reader to infer the significance of the change in control of the manna produced by the different voting rules.

For Buchanan, then, the self-interest assumption does not imply any substantive content, although it is also assumed that individuals cannot pursue an objective public interest because such an objective public interest does not exist. Hence, conflict between the values and ends of different individuals is always possible, but that value-conflict could be between different other-regarding priorities (e.g. between increasing the welfare payments made to pensioners or to single mothers) or between different self-serving ends (e.g. between the demands of different producer interests). As discussed in Chapter 2, Buchanan has argued that there are reasons to believe that self-serving individuals are likely to prosper in the political realm (e.g. RoR, Chapter 4), but the possibility that altruistic individuals will rise to the top in politics is not discounted and does not change the basic analysis.

Rationality

A third principal assumption of Buchanan's work that has been subject to widespread criticism is that of individual rationality. According to Buchanan, individuals are assumed to be rational utility-maximizers, meaning that people will always act in accordance with their own self-conceived ends.

As described in Chapter 2, like the self-interest assumption, the rationality assumption is said to contain no substantive content, so that, for example, if the members of a primordial tribe believed that sacrificing animals would please the gods and make the forests plentiful it would be perfectly rational for them to do so, however 'irrational' such behaviour may appear to people outside the tribe (e.g. CoC, Chapter 4; MSMO, pp. 55–70).

The rationality assumption has been criticized on the grounds that it provides a partial or misleading account of human behaviour. Perhaps the most celebrated critique of the rationality assumption in contemporary economics (which would logically also apply to public choice theory) was written by Nobel laureate Amartya Sen (1978). In his essay on 'rational fools', Sen argued that the rationality assumption neglects the complex psychological issues that underlie human choices. In particular, individuals may be subject to varying and conflicting desires and demands, and how people choose to make sense of, balance and ultimately satisfy these different desires and demands may alter from day to day. According to Self (1993, p. 9), then, the 'concept of rationality can be criticized as narrow, one-dimensional and short-sighted. It does not delve into the deeper roots of individual behaviour'.

In reality, Buchanan's work has always stressed the importance of understanding individual choices as inherently personal, subjective and complex. Indeed, a principal theme of his book *Cost and Choice*, perhaps Buchanan's most important contribution to economic theory, was that the opportunity costs of any decision were knowable only to the individual concerned and therefore could not be aggregated to produce objective comparisons of social welfare resulting from different collective decisions; a person observing the choosing individual could not know the calculus of personal costs and benefits that had led him or her to make a particular choice.

For Buchanan, the notion that individual choices are inherently personal, complex and subjective is entirely compatible with the idea that individuals are rational actors. According to Buchanan, the rationality assumption simply implies that individuals will want more of what they consider to be good and less of what they consider to be bad; it says nothing about the substantive content of possible goods and bads, nor how people decide which phenomena fall into each category (MSMO, pp. 58–63).

The value of the rationality assumption in Buchanan's work lies in its ability to illuminate the impact of different institutions on individual choice. The insight that a rational individual with stable preferences may choose differently in the marketplace and in the political sphere is one of the most important scholarly contributions of public choice theory that has added significantly to knowledge about the relationship between individuals and institutions. Without the rationality assumption, this insight would not be apparent: differences in individual choices in different institutional contexts might instead be attributable to irrational behaviour producing intransitive preferences.

Unanimity

A fourth foundational assumption of Buchanan's work that has been challenged by the critics of public choice theory is the postulation that constitutional agreement should be unanimous and that deviations from unanimity in post-constitutional decision-making must be themselves unanimously agreed. As described in Chapter 2, for Buchanan, people cannot involuntarily enter into a social contract, therefore, in constitutional agreement, 'there is *no* place for majority rule or, indeed, for any rule short of unanimity' (CCC, p. 220). At the post-constitutional level, however, it is recognized that the principle of unanimity would frustrate purposeful collective action and therefore it is argued that rational individuals would choose to utilize a less stringent decision-making rule in post-constitutional politics (e.g. CoC, Chapter 7; LoL, Chapters 4 and 5).

Shapiro (1990; 1996) has criticized the use of the principle of unanimity in the work of Buchanan and other public choice theorists as inherently conservative. For Shapiro, the principle of unanimity privileges the status quo by giving each individual the power of veto over every political decision and thereby making any political change or reform almost impossible to achieve.

According to Shapiro (1996, pp. 227–229), constitutional political economy mistakenly presents politics as a series of consensual moves leading to the creation of political institutions where none previously existed, when in fact there is scant evidence that real world political institutions have been created via the unanimous consent of the governed, and, if this did happen, 'whatever contractualist element these arrangements once exhibited has receded into the mists of time' (Shapiro, 1996, p. 229). Shapiro argues that when politics is analysed from a non-contractarian perspective, majority rule under conditions of universal suffrage can be seen as a political ideal, precisely because it enables the majority 'to dispossess a minority of ill-gotten gains' (Shapiro, 1996, p. 17). According to Shapiro, although the principle of unanimity is presented as a means of protecting individual liberty, it is in fact an inherently conservative element in Buchanan's thought that serves to protect the interest of a fortunate minority by blocking the possibility of radical redistributive politics.

The principle of unanimity is said to privilege the status quo in the constitutional agreement because it is only deviations *from* the status quo that actually require unanimous consent. It is argued that positive agreement will not be required to assign post-constitutional legal status to property holdings that pre-date the social contract, whereas demands to redistribute income and wealth as part of a constitutional agreement will require such positive agreement; it is therefore claimed that the former but not the latter is likely to be part of a unanimously agreed constitution (Shapiro 1990; 1996, Chapter 2).

It is true that in Buchanan's model of the social contract the contracting parties do not begin from a blank slate, but are conceptualized in a state of nature where some individuals have possession of more wealth than others. Moreover, this inequality may have arisen as a result of violent predation by the strong against the weak. Constitutional agreement, then, has to be reached among unequal individuals; the rich and the poor, the powerful and the powerless, must unanimously agree to the same constitutional settlement. Both Buchanan and Shapiro would agree that such a contract is likely to involve legal recognition of (most if not all) existing property claims and thereby the legitimization of holdings that have been obtained via predation.

What Shapiro fails to recognize, however, is that this can only happen if it is in the interests of every individual, including the least advantaged. If the weak and the poor could organize collectively in the state of nature to recoup their losses from the rich and the powerful, then they would not gain from entering into the social contract and logically would not do so. The social contract involves leaving the state of nature so that predation can cease and everyone can enjoy the benefits of peace and mutual disarmament.

In Shapiro's non-contractarian conception of 'democracy', where there is no social contract, people effectively do not leave the state of nature. Rather, Shapiro sees democracy as a continuation of predation by other means. By rejecting the principle of unanimity in constitutional contract, Shapiro advocates a politics in which property rights are in constant threat of predation from organized groups that capture the political process, a situation Buchanan has characterized as 'constitutional anarchy'. Moreover, Shapiro does not appear to consider the possibility that the least advantaged will be the least able to organize politically and therefore it is they who will be the most vulnerable in the constitutional anarchy he advocates.

Shapiro's argument, then, is based upon a conceptualization of politics as an inherently conflictual activity where Pareto improvements (where no person is made worse off and at least one person is made better off) are almost impossible to achieve (Shapiro, 1996, pp. 20–21). Buchanan, likewise, sees non-contractual politics as inherently conflictual, but this leads him to argue for constitutionalism and for limits to the scope of the political realm so that wherever possible goods and services are provided via the market where exchanges are based on the principle of mutual advantage and Pareto improvements are the norm (e.g. FLL, pp. 68–70).

The crucial difference between Buchanan and Shapiro, then, turns upon Buchanan's insight that the poor are worse off in both anarchy and constitutional anarchy, compared to a unanimously agreed constitutional order that has given legitimacy and protection to the property of the rich and the poor (LoL, Chapter 4). Shapiro seems to be unaware that this conclusion follows logically from the application of the principle of unanimity in constitutional choice; it is only in the absence of unanimity that we cannot say with certainty that everyone will be better off in the post-constitutional situation.

Furthermore, it is not the case that the application of the principle of unanimity to real world post-constitutional politics necessarily has conservative implications. As set out in the previous chapter, Buchanan shows that applying the principle of unanimity to contemporary politics raises the difficult question of whether people would unanimously agree to the institutional arrangements that exist in contemporary democracies. In particular, would the poor in contemporary America or Britain unanimously agree to the political, economic and social arrangements within which they presently live if those arrangements were presented as a constitutional choice? The principle of unanimity may give the rich a veto over radical reform, but, contra Shapiro, when applied in this way it also gives the poor a veto over the status quo. The challenge of constitutional political economy is to discover institutional arrangements that can command the unanimous consent of the governed, rich and poor, strong and weak, advantaged and less-advantaged (LoL, Chapter 10; RoR, Chapter 9).

Power

The fifth and final foundational critique of public choice theory to be considered in this chapter is the claim that public choice neglects the issue of power. According to Udehn (1996, p. 206): 'The absence of power is a serious deficiency in the positive and normative versions of public choice alike'.

Public choice theory is said to lack an account of power because public choice theorists model politics as a form of exchange. It is claimed that neoclassical economics fallaciously models economic exchange as free from power relations and that, 'Public choice, at least as a theory of exchange, is equally devoid of a theory of power' (Udehn, 1996, p. 161).

It is certainly true that both neoclassical economics and public choice theory begin from idealized conceptions of economics and politics as consensual enterprises within which people voluntarily come together to achieve mutually advantageous ends. In the economic marketplace people trade goods and services for mutual advantage; in the political realm people come together to overcome collective action problems that may not be solvable in private markets. In both contexts, however, the exchange model is essentially an ideal against which to compare real world practice.

Hence, neoclassical economics may be characterized as the study of market failure and, moreover, many of the market failures that detain neoclassical economists result from what are essentially unequal power relationships, such as problems of asymmetrical information and the existence of monopolies.

Similarly, while public choice theory begins with an idealized model of politics as exchange, the account of the pathologies of majoritarian democracy in the work of Buchanan and others is centred on the question of power. Hence, the public choice critique of majoritarian democracy is focused upon the fact that political power has a strong potential to be used for exploitative ends. As Buchanan and Tullock (CoC, p. 89) put it: 'the essence of the collective-choice process under majority voting rules is the fact that the minority of voters are forced to accede to actions which they cannot prevent and for which they cannot claim compensation for damages resulting'. In other words, the *essence* of majoritarian politics is the possibility of minority exploitation.

Indeed, as discussed in Chapter 2, Brennan and Buchanan (RoR, p. 72) likened political power to an economic monopoly that is auctioned to the highest bidder and tends to attract those for whom power will bring the greatest rewards. Such a view clearly implies a conception of both economic and political power.

It is not the case, then, that public choice theory does not engage with the concept of power. On the contrary, public choice theory is first and foremost an account of the sources of and the remedies to the problem of political power. At the centre of Buchanan's work is an account of the role of unanimously agreed constitutional rules as the only effective solution to the arbitrary exercise of political power.

In summary, the critics of Buchanan's work and public choice theory more generally have tended not to engage with the substantive conclusions of the sub-discipline. It is generally accepted that those conclusions follow logically from the analytical approach of public choice theory. Rather, it is the fundamental assumptions underlying public choice theory that have been the principal object of critique. This section has attempted to show that these critiques have not been successful and have tended to demonstrate a failure to fully appreciate the nuances of the public choice approach on the part of its critics.

The Development of Public Choice as an Academic Community

When Buchanan and a small number of colleagues established the political economy research centre at the University of Virginia at Charlottesville in 1957 it was the only academic centre in the world dedicated to the systematic application of economic ideas to political decision-making. There were only a handful of scholars involved in similar work at other academic institutions and many of them were to move to the Center for Study of Public Choice as it relocated to Blacksburg and then to Fairfax in Virginia.

Today the Center for Study of Public Choice continues to thrive at George Mason University, but now it is one of a number of similar research centres at universities around the world from the University of Turku in Finland to the Universidad Francisco Marroquín in Guatemala. In addition to these specialist public choice research centres that now exist, today almost every economics department in the world will employ teachers and researchers with expertise in public choice theory.

The Public Choice Society emerged from a conference organised by Buchanan and Gordon Tullock in 1963 as an informal society to facilitate the exchange of ideas among scholars working in the sub-discipline. The Society has grown into one of the largest groupings of academics in the social sciences, with hundreds of scholars from many different countries attending its annual meetings. Three winners of the Nobel Prize in Economics have served as presidents of the Public Choice Society: Buchanan, Vernon Smith (2002 Nobel Prize laureate) and Elinor Ostrom (2009 Nobel Prize laureate).[1]

There are now two peer-review learned journals dedicated to the publication of public choice scholarship. The journal *Public Choice*, originally established as *Papers on Non-Market Decision-Making* in 1966 under the editorship of Gordon Tullock, has now become a leading peer-review outlet for public choice work, consistently attaining an impact factor (the measure of a journal's impact based on the citations of work published therein) that places it among the most prestigious economic and political science journals.

Since 1990 *Public Choice* has been complemented by *Constitutional Political Economy*, established under the editorship of two of Buchanan's co-authors, Viktor J. Vanberg and Richard E. Wagner. *Constitutional Political Economy* has not attained the same high impact factor achieved by *Public Choice*, but it has nevertheless become an important scholarly outlet for work in the public choice sub-discipline.

Although Buchanan may be described as the leading researcher in the field of public choice, it is probably accurate to say that much work published in the sub-discipline and in the journal *Public Choice* is some distance removed from Buchanan's own approach to the study of political decision-making. While much of Buchanan's output is highly theoretical, dealing with abstract analysis of idealized models of individual choice in different institutional settings, Buchanan has nevertheless eschewed the formal mathematical modelling that has become the norm in much contemporary economic analysis. Indeed, Buchanan's work may be understood as an attempt to return economics to its origins as an enterprise in moral philosophy. However, a significant proportion of the scholars working in the sub-discipline and publishing in the journal *Public Choice* engage in formal mathematical modelling of political decision-making that is quite different to Buchanan's more nuanced, institutional approach.

Public choice theory has also had a direct impact on the real world of policy and politics. As Roger Congleton (2002), another of Buchanan's co-authors and a Director of the Center for Study of Public Choice at Fairfax, has written, following the collapse of Communist regimes in Eastern Europe and Africa public choice scholars were often instrumental in the creation of new democratic constitutions that sought to limit government and ensure fiscal responsibility. Public choice scholars have also served in the US government, most notably James C. Miller III, a graduate of the Center who was Chair of the US Federal Trade Commission from 1981 to 1985 and Director of the US Office of Management and Budget from 1985 to 1988. Buchanan and other public choice scholars have also been invited to testify before the US Congress on tax and other matters, although Buchanan has expressed strong scepticism with regard to economists assuming the role of advisor to government: 'Government, or politics, was, to me, always something to seek protection from, not something to exploit, either for my own ends or those that I might define for the public at large' (EFTOI, p. 97).

It is impossible, of course, to definitively isolate and thereby measure the precise influence of Buchanan on the development of public choice as a sub-discipline and/or as an academic community. As Congleton has put it, 'Whether or not there would have been a Virginia School of political economy without James Buchanan can be debated, but that his work and leadership at UVA, VPI and GMU played an important role in its development and direction cannot' (Congleton, 2002, p. 27).

Hence, although public choice may have been an archetypal 'idea waiting to happen', there is no doubt that Buchanan was the key figure in making the idea happen at the time that it did and that the development of the sub-discipline in the second half of the twentieth century bears the indelible imprint of his remarkable intellectual vision.

Notes

[1] Further information on the Public Choice Society can be found on the organisation's web pages at: http://www.pubchoicesoc.org/index.html.

Chapter 4

The Continuing and Future Relevance of Buchanan's Ideas

The previous three chapters of this book have provided an intellectual biography of James M. Buchanan, set out Buchanan's ideas in some detail, and considered the influence and reception of those ideas. This short, final chapter will consider the continuing and future relevance of Buchanan's work and ideas.

Buchanan's work is principally concerned with the pathologies and the possibilities of democratic politics. For Buchanan, the democratic ideal of self-government – the belief that all individuals should have the power to frame and pursue their own ends – is a noble one. Buchanan's belief in the nobility of democracy properly understood as individual self-government is based upon his adherence to the basic Kantian premise that each individual must be respected as a unique sovereign agent. As Buchanan (LFCL, p. 288) has described: 'Individuals are to be allowed to choose among potentially available alternatives simply because they are the ultimate sovereigns'.

It is worth emphasizing that the notion that every individual should have the power to frame and pursue his or her own ends does not imply that each person has a right to do whatever he or she wishes irrespective of the impact of his or her actions on others, or that individuals should have the power to compel others to serve their ends. Rather, Buchanan's conception of individual empowerment implies that people should be free to reach accommodations between their ends and the ends of others that are not dictated by external authority, but reflect their own subjective perceptions of the costs and benefits of alternative courses of action.

For Buchanan, it is bilateral exchanges based on the principle of mutual advantage in the marketplace that provide the ideal model for democratic politics: 'The simple exchange of apples and oranges between two traders – this institutional model is the starting point for all that I have done' (LFCL, p. 26). For Buchanan, both economic and political decision-making should be processes of exchange within which people seek to reconcile their often conflicting and incommensurable ends to mutual advantage.

In contemporary democratic polities, however, democracy has very often become the process by which individual ends are subjugated to the ends of others. Unconstrained majoritarian democracy enables a majority of the electorate to impose its wishes on a minority that has no means of escape or amelioration. Moreover, the vagaries of democratic decision-making mean that very often organized minorities are able to capture the political process and impose their wishes on the majority.

Consequently, in a contemporary democracy many people will have to work to pay for goods and services that they do not wish to purchase, or be required to purchase goods and services in quantities that they would not have chosen independently. So many goods and services are now provided via the political process that the citizens of democratic states spend between a third and a half of their working lives labouring to pay taxes many of which they would not voluntarily choose to pay. Herein lies the incongruity between the ideal of individual self-government and the practical reality of modern democracy: for all the rhetoric of democratic empowerment today people are less free than at almost any point in the past in terms of their ability to spend their income and wealth in pursuit of the ends that they consider the most important.

Concerns about popular discontent with democracy have become commonplace in the academic literature in recent years. There is strong empirical evidence of declining trust in democratic institutions in all the advanced democracies, as evidenced by declining rates of political participation, falling voter turnout, reduced membership of political parties and dwindling knowledge of democratic politics, (e.g. Dalton, 2004; Newton, 2006; Putnam, 2000).

Anyone familiar with Buchanan's work and public choice theory more generally will not be surprised by the decline of popular faith in democracy given the inability of democratic institutions as presently constituted to effectively respond to people's preferences. When people are accustomed to participating in a market economy that facilitates and satisfies a huge range and diversity of choices it is little wonder that participation in the democratic process, where the possibility of receiving the goods and services that one wants in the quantities one desires is extremely slim, will seem constraining and disempowering by comparison.

For many contemporary scholars declining popular satisfaction with democracy seems to necessitate government intervention to create the necessary civic culture to enable democracy to flourish (e.g. Dalton, 2004; Newton, 2006; Putnam, 2000). But there is scant evidence that increasing the scope of government in such a way will end public disaffection with democratic institutions. On the contrary, the public choice analysis exemplified in Buchanan's work would suggest that such an approach will only heighten the failings of democracy by increasing the size of the political realm and thereby increasing the proportion of goods and services provided in quantities other than those that individuals would themselves choose.

Buchanan's solution to the problems facing contemporary democracies is to reduce the scope of government via constitutional limits on government power. It is argued that an effectively constrained democracy may be capable of realizing the promise of individual self-government.

For Buchanan, a constitution describes unanimously agreed and respected rules and conventions that govern what government can and cannot do. Anything less than unanimous agreement means that at least one individual will be forced to abide by rules to which he or she has not consented and is therefore incompatible with the principle of self-government. Among the decisions made at the constitutional level will be the selection of the non-unanimous, qualified majority voting rules that will govern post-constitutional political decision-making.

Buchanan (PFDP, p. 302) has argued that without reform to denormalize the use of the political process as a means of extracting wealth from others the future of democracy is bleak and, moreover, it deserves to be bleak: 'if individuals come to consider governmental processes as nothing more than available means through which separate coalitions can exploit each other, democracy cannot, and should not, survive'.

It seems reasonable to predict that the salience of Buchanan's analysis of democracy will increase in the future. The twentieth century saw the spread of democracy from Western Europe and North America to large parts of the world, including countries in Eastern and Central Europe, South America, Asia and Africa. In the early years of the twenty-first century democratic states undertook military action to install nominally democratic regimes in Iraq and Afghanistan at enormous human cost to all concerned. Democratization has often been accompanied by tremendous hopes of popular emancipation and citizen empowerment. But Buchanan's analysis suggests that there is little reason to believe that the new democracies will succeed where the old democracies have failed. On the contrary, the public choice account of democracy suggests that the high hopes of the citizens of the new democracies are unlikely to be fulfilled.

According to Buchanan, in the absence of effective constitutional constraints, majoritarian democracy is likely to lead to the subjugation of some people to the will of others and hence something akin to a continuation of the tyrannies that people hoped democracy would end.

There are good reasons, then, to believe that Buchanan's work will gain in salience in the years ahead as one of the most powerful explanations of the failure of democratic politics to realize its promise and also one of the most cogent proposals for reform in order to realize the democratic ideal of individual self-government. As long as unconstrained democracy exists as a dominant form of government throughout the world, Buchanan's work will retain its relevance for scholars and policymakers alike.

Bibliography

For an explanation of the referencing conventions for Buchanan's works, please refer to the explanatory note at the beginning of the book.

Arrow, Kenneth J. (1951) *Social Choice and Individual Values*, New Haven: Yale University Press.
Barber, James D. (1965) *The Lawmakers: Recruitment and Adaption to Legislative Life*, New Haven: Yale University Press.
Black, Duncan (1958) *The Theory of Committees and Elections*, Cambridge: Cambridge University Press.
Boettke, Peter J. (1998) 'James M. Buchanan and the Rebirth of Political Economy', in Steve Pressman and Ric Holt, eds, *Against the Grain: Dissent in Economics*, Cheltenham, UK: Edward Elgar.
Boyd, Richard (1997) 'Introduction' in Frank H. Knight, *The Ethics of Competition*, New Brunswick, NJ.: Transaction Publishers.
Brennan, Geoffrey (2004) 'Life in the Putty Knife Factory!' *American Journal of Economics and Sociology*, 63, 1, pp. 79–104.
Brennan, Geoffrey and Buchanan, James M. (1980 [2000]) *The Power to Tax*, Indianapolis: Liberty Fund.
— (1985 [2000]) *The Reason of Rules*, Indianapolis: Liberty Fund.
Buchanan, James M. (1958 [1999]) *Public Principles of Public Debt*, Indianapolis: Liberty Fund.
— (1967 [1999]) *Public Finance in Democratic Process*, Indianapolis: Liberty Fund.
— (1968 [1999]) *The Demand and Supply of Public Goods*, Indianapolis: Liberty Fund.
— (1969 [1999]) *Cost and Choice*, Indianapolis: Liberty Fund.
— (1975 [1999]) *The Limits of Liberty*, Indianapolis: Liberty Fund.

— (1998) *The Logical Foundations of Constitutional Liberty*, Indianapolis: Liberty Fund.
— (2000) *Economic Inquiry and Its Logic*, Indianapolis: Liberty Fund.
— (2000) *Politics as Public Choice*, Indianapolis: Liberty Fund.
— (2000) *Debt and Taxes*, Indianapolis: Liberty Fund.
— (2001) *Externalities and Public Expenditure Theory*, Indianapolis: Liberty Fund.
— (2001) *Choice, Contract and Constitutions*, Indianapolis: Liberty Fund.
— (2001) *Moral Science and Moral Order*, Indianapolis: Liberty Fund.
— (2001) *Federalism, Liberty, and the Law*, Indianapolis: Liberty Fund.
— (2001) *Ideas, Persons and Events*, Indianapolis: Liberty Fund.
— (2005) *Why I, Too, Am Not a Conservative*, Cheltenham, UK: Edward Elgar.
— (2007) *Economics from the Outside In*, College Station, Texas: A&M University Press.
Buchanan, James M. and Congleton, Roger D. (1998 [2003]) *Politics by Principle, Not Interest*, Indianapolis: Liberty Fund.
Buchanan, James M. and Devletoglou, Nicos E. (1971) *Academia in Anarchy*, London: Tom Stacey.
Buchanan, James M. and Musgrave, Richard A. (1999) *Public Finance and Public Choice: Two Contrasting Visions of the State*, Cambridge, MA: MIT Press.
Buchanan, James M. and Tullock, Gordon (1962 [1999]) *The Calculus of Consent*, Indianapolis: Liberty Fund.
Bush, Winston C. (1972) 'Individual Welfare in Anarchy', in Gordon Tullock, ed., *Explorations in the Theory of Anarchy*, Blacksburg, VA: Center for Study of Public Choice.
Coase, Ronald A. (1960) 'The problem of social cost', *Journal of Law and Economics*, 3, pp. 1–44.
Condorcet, Marquis de (1785) *Essay on the Application of Analysis to the Probability of Majority Decisions*, Paris: De L'Imprimerie Royale.
Congleton, Roger (2002) 'Buchanan and the Virginia School', in Geoffrey Brennan, Hartmut Kliemt and Robert D. Tollison, eds, *Methods and Morals in Constitutional Economics*, Berlin: Springer.

Dalton, Russell J. (2004) *Democratic Challenges Democratic Choices*, Oxford: Oxford University Press.

Downs, Anthony (1957) *An Economic Theory of Democracy*, New York: Addison-Wesley.

— (1964) 'Review: *The Calculus of Consent*', *Journal of Political Economy*, 72, 1, pp. 87–88.

Dunleavy, Patrick (1991) *Democracy, Bureaucracy and Public Choice: Economic Explanations in Political Science*, Hemel Hempstead: Harvester Wheatsheaf.

Friedman, Jeffrey (1996) 'Introduction: Economic Approaches to Politics', in Jeffrey Friedman, ed., *The Rational Choice Controversy*, New Haven: Yale University Press.

Goodin, Robert and Le Grand, Julian (1987) *Not Only the Poor: The Middle Classes and the Welfare State*, London: Allen and Unwin.

Gordon, Scott (1976) 'The New Contractarians', *Journal of Political Economy*, 84, 3, pp. 573–590.

Green, Donald P. and Shapiro, Ian (1994) *Pathologies of Rational Choice Theory*, New Haven: Yale University Press.

Hayek, F. A. (1944) *The Road to Serfdom*, London: Routledge.

— (1960) *The Constitution of Liberty*, London: Routledge.

Hobbes, Thomas (1651 [1982]) *Leviathan*, London: Penguin Classics.

Horn, Karen Ilse (2009) *Roads to Wisdom: Conversations with Ten Nobel Laureates in Economics*, Cheltenham, UK: Edward Elgar.

Hume, David (1777 [1963]) 'Of the Independency of Parliament', in *Essays Moral, Political and Literary*, Oxford: Oxford University Press.

Johnson, Marianne (2006) 'The Wicksellian Unanimity Rule: The Competing Interpretations of Buchanan and Musgrave', *Journal of the History of Economic Thought*, 28, 1, pp. 57–78.

Kelman, Mark (1988) 'On Democracy-Bashing: A Skeptical Look at the Theoretical and "Empirical" Practice of the Public Choice Movement', *Virginia Law Review*, 74, 2, pp. 199–273.

Krueger, Anne O. (1974) 'The Political Economy of the Rent-Seeking Society', *American Economic Review*, 63, 3, pp. 291–303.

Kurrild-Klitgaard, Peter (2001) 'An empirical example of the Condorcet paradox of voting in a large electorate', *Public Choice*, 107, pp. 135–145.

Mack, Eric (2009) *John Locke*, New York: Continuum.
Meadowcroft, John (2001) 'Political Recruitment and Local Representation: The Case of Liberal Democract Councillors', *Local Government Studies*, 27, 1, pp. 19–36.
McDonald. Michael D. and Budge, Ian (2006) *Elections, Parties, Democracy*, Oxford: Oxford University Press.
McKenzie, Richard B. (2004) 'The Importance of Deviance in Intellectual Development: Especially at Virginia Tech in the 1970s', *American Journal of Economics and Sociology*, 63, 1, pp. 19–49.
Newton, Kenneth (2006) 'Political Support: Social Capital, Civil Society and Political and Economic Performance', *Political Studies*, 54, pp. 846–864.
Nozick, Robert (1974) *Anarchy, State, and Utopia*, New York: Basic Books.
Petracca, Mark P. (1991) 'The Rational Actor Approach to Politics: Science, Self-Interest, and Normative Democratic Theory', in Kristen Renwick Monroe, ed., *The Economic Approach to Politics: A Critical Reassessment of the Theory of Rational Action*, New York: HarperCollins.
Putnam, Robert D. (2000) *Bowling Alone: The Collapse and Revival of American Community*, New York: Simon and Schuster.
Rao, Nirmala (1998) 'The Recruitment of Representatives in British Local Government: Pathways and Barriers', *Policy and Politics*, 26, 3, pp. 291–305.
Rawls, John (1971) *A Theory of Justice*, Cambridge, MA: Harvard University Press.
Reisman, David (1990) *The Political Economy of James Buchanan*, College Station, TX: Texas A&M University Press.
Romer, Thomas (1988) 'Nobel Laureate: On James Buchanan's Contributions to Economics', *Journal of Economic Perspectives*, 2, 4, pp. 165–179.
Self, Peter (1993) *Government by the Market? The Politics of Public Choice*, Basingstoke: Macmillan.
Sen, Amartya K. (1978) 'Rational Fools: A Critique of the Behavioural Foundations of Economic Theory', in H. Harris, ed., *Scientific Models and Men*, London: Oxford University Press.
Shapiro, Ian (1990) 'Three Fallacies Concerning Majorities, Minorities and Democratic Policies', in John W. Chapman

and Alan Wertheimer, eds, *NOMOS XXXII: Majorities and Minorities*, New York: New York University Press.
— (1996) *Democracy's Place*, Ithaca: Cornell University Press.
Stringham, Edward, ed., (2005) *Anarchy, State and Public Choice*, Cheltenham, UK: Edward Elgar.
Summers, Adam B. (2009) *California Spending by the Numbers: A Historic Look at State Spending from Gov Pete Wilson to Gov Arnold Schwarzenegger*, Los Angeles, CA.: Reason Foundation.
Tiebout, Charles M. (1956) 'A Pure Theory of Local Expenditure', *Journal of Political Economy*, 64, 5, pp. 416–424.
Tullock, Gordon (1967) 'Welfare Costs of Tariffs, Monopolies and Theft', *Western Economic Journal*, 5, 3, pp. 224–232.
— (1974) *The Social Dilemma: The Economics of War and Redistribution*, Blacksburg, VA: Center for Study of Public Choice.
Tullock, Gordon, ed., (1972) *Explorations in the Theory of Anarchy*, Blacksburg, VA: Center for Study of Public Choice.
— (1974) *Further Explorations in the Theory of Anarchy*, Blacksburg, VA: Center for Study of Public Choice.
Udehn, Lars (1996) *The Limits of Public Choice: A sociological critique of the economic theory of politics*, London: Routledge.
Wicksell, Knut (1896 [1994]) 'A New Principle of Just Taxation', trans. James M. Buchanan, in Richard A. Musgrave and Alan T. Peacock, eds, *Classics in the Theory of Public Finance*, Basingstoke: Palgrave Macmillan.

Index

Academia in Anarchy (Buchanan
and Devletoglou) 27
Allais, Maurice 21
Allen, Clark 17
altruism 15, 42, 56, 145, 146,
148 *see also* benevolence;
motivational symmetry;
self-interest
*American Political Science
Review* 133
anarchy 25–7, 29–31, 36,
45–50, 51, 52, 59, 107
constitutional
anarchy 63–107, 128–9,
153
see also state of nature
Arrow, Kenneth 17
Article 13 (California) 111–12

benevolence 13, 18, 92 *see also*
altruism; motivational
symmetry; self-interest
Black, Duncan 21, 131
Boettke, Peter J. 139
Brennan, Geoffrey 28, 42, 46,
47, 51, 54, 69, 75, 91, 92,
96, 106, 110, 111, 112, 113,
114, 115, 123, 124, 138
Buchanan, James M.
childhood 4–5

conservatism 129–30, 151–5
democratic values 17, 22,
29, 35, 40–2, 45, 55, 61,
105, 124, 161–2
education 5–16
family 4–5, 33
Italian year 18–19
Nobel Prize acceptance
speech 14–15
Nobel Prize award 1, 4,
14–15, 32–3, 133
outsider to mainstream
academic/political
culture 4–5, 6–7, 10,
23–7, 32, 159–60
PhD thesis 15
socialist beliefs (and their
correction) 8–10
war service 6–7
working practices 28, 33
Buchanan, John P.
(grandfather of James M.
Buchanan) 5
bureaucracy/bureaucrats 13,
21, 45, 64, 72, 97–8,
101–4, 114–15, 124, 135
Bush, Winston C. 29–30, 34

Calculus of Consent, The
(Buchanan and

Index

Tullock) 2, 21, 22, 26, 37–8, 58, 67, 85–6, 88, 120–1, 130–1, 135, 137, 147
Chicago public choice 19–20
see also University of Chicago
Coase, Ronald 21, 128
coercion 13, 48–50, 60, 82–106
Colberg, Marshall 17
collective choices 17, 18, 22, 29, 37, 54, 55, 57–9, 64, 65–82, 85–6, 98–9, 114, 150, 151, 156
Condorcet, Marquis de 66
Congleton, Roger 41, 82, 85, 117–20, 159, 160
consent 14, 26, 30, 46, 53–4, 56, 64, 66, 82–4, 108, 116, 125, 151–2, 154, 164
Constitution 1, 14, 19–20, 22–3, 25, 26, 32, 35, 36, 37, 45, 52–6, 57, 59, 60–3, 64–5, 71, 77, 83, 85, 90, 107–29, 130–1, 138, 141–2, 151–4, 156, 159, 164
constitutional anarchy 63–107, 128–9, 153
constitutional revolution 123–9
constitutionalism 57, 107–29, 153
fiscal constitution 14, 110–29
formal and informal 109
US constitution 22–3, 25, 26, 32

Constitutional Political Economy (journal) 158
contract/contractarianism *see* constitution; social contract
Cost and Choice (Buchanan) 150

De Viti De Marco, Antonio 18
decision-making costs 58–9, 83
democracy 11, 22–3, 37, 40–1, 60–3, 65–82, 85, 88–90, 92, 98, 103, 105, 107, 116, 119–20, 125, 128, 130, 132, 153, 156, 161–5
democratization 164–5
Devletoglou, Nicos 26
Downs, Anthony 70, 135
Dunleavy, Patrick 134

ethical individualism 37, 40, 124–5, 143–4
exchange
  economic (in markets) 52–4, 154–6, 162
  political 15, 52–4, 126–8, 154–6, 162
exploitation 13–14, 32, 37, 65, 82–92, 94, 107, 110–11, 121, 140, 156
  see also external costs
external costs 37, 58–9, 65, 82–92, 106 *see also* exploitation

fairness 6–7, 13, 57
federalism 15, 121–3
Florida State University at Tallahassee 16–17

Friedman, Jeffrey 146
Friedman, Milton 9

Generality Principle,
 The 116–19
government, growth of 56,
 83–4, 96–107, 111–12
Green, Donald P. 133

Hayek, F. A. 21, 91, 129, 130
Hobbes, Thomas 15, 45, 47,
 52, 65, 86, 96, 106
human nature 46–7, 90–2
Hume, David 47, 92

individualism *see*
 methodological
 individualism; ethical
 individualism
inequality 48–50, 125–8,
 152–5
Italian public finance 3,
 18–19

Journal of Political Economy 17
justice 7, 13, 14
 distributive justice 86, 96
 racial justice 25
Juvenal 97

Kant, Immanuel 40, 42, 161
Kelman, Mark 3, 22
Kennedy, John F. 23
Keynes, John M. 113
Knight, Frank 3, 8–11, 15, 16,
 21, 36
knowledge problems
 (in politics) 12, 69–71
Krueger, Anne O. 92

legitimacy 45–7, 56, 63, 65,
 66, 67, 83, 105–6, 117,
 123, 126, 154
Liberty Fund 27, 33, 133
Limits of Liberty, The (Buchanan)
 15, 30, 37, 99, 131
Leoni, Bruno 21
Locke, John 15, 45, 50
London School of
 Economics 26

Mack, Eric 51
Madison, James 22–3, 32, 130
majority rule 13–14, 54, 58–9,
 65–6, 67, 80–3, 85–90, 91,
 95, 109, 119–21, 122, 132,
 137, 151–2, 162, 164
market, the 8–10, 28, 38–9,
 128, 135, 142
 compared to politics 1–3,
 17, 52–3, 61–2, 68–74,
 78–81, 82, 92–3, 95, 102,
 104–5, 107, 114, 121–2,
 135, 137–8, 145, 150,
 154–5, 162–3
market failure 128, 139–40,
 155–6
median voter theory 65–6
methodological
 individualism 12, 15,
 18, 22, 36, 37–45, 129,
 141–5
 in Buchanan's critique of
 Arrow 17
Middle Tennessee Teachers
 College 4, 5, 7–8
Miller, James C. III 159
minority rule 88–90, 98, 122,
 132, 152

motivational symmetry 15, 22, 42–3, 90–2, 136–7, 145–9
Murfreesboro, TN 5–6

neutrality 39–42, 60–3 *see also* Generality Principle, The
New Institutional Economics 138
Nixon, Richard 24, 159
Nobel Prize in Economic Sciences 1, 4, 14–15, 21, 32–3, 133, 149, 158
non-discriminatory politics *see* Generality Principle, The
Nozick, Robert 45, 51
Nutter, Warren G. 20–1, 24

Ostrom, Elinor 158

Petracca, Mark, P. 22, 141, 146
Polanyi, Michael 21
political decision-making *see* collective choices; democracy; voting
power 14, 22, 25, 48–50, 52, 53, 54, 57, 64–5, 82–92, 97, 103–5, 106, 108, 109, 110, 114–15, 116, 129, 140, 151, 152, 153, 155–7, 161–5
Prada 43, 145
prices/price theory 8–9, 10, 38, 55, 64, 68, 73, 93
Public Choice (journal) 158–9
Public Choice Society, The 157–8, 160

public choice theory 1–4, 14–15, 17, 22, 34, 63, 133–40, 157–60
 critics of 22, 140–57
 as moral philosophy 20, 159
public debt 18–19, 44–5, 76–7, 87–8, 113
public goods 37, 46, 56–60, 74, 78–9, 83–6, 96, 98, 104–5, 107, 118–19, 121–2
Public Principles of Public Debt (Buchanan) 18–19, 44–5, 87
Putnam, Robert D. 163

rational ignorance 70–1
rationality/rational choice 30, 43–4, 49, 50, 57, 59, 74, 94, 98, 113, 121, 129, 133, 135, 136, 138, 142–3, 149–50
 see also transitive/intransitive preferences
Rawls, John 45, 51, 55, 131
rent-seeking 37, 65, 92–6, 106, 118, 140
 costs of 94–6
Rice University 24
rights 25, 36, 48–50, 50–2, 64, 84–6, 96, 102, 106, 108, 109, 116, 129
 natural rights 36, 50–2
 property rights 29–30, 54, 56, 59, 61, 63, 64, 105, 126–9, 153–4
Rousseau, Jean-Jacques 15, 45

Index

Self, Peter 3, 22, 145, 149
self-interest 22, 30, 42–3, 83, 135–6, 138, 145–9 *see also* altruism; benevolence; motivational symmetry
Sen, Amartya 149
Shapiro, Ian 3, 22, 133, 151–5
Sims, C. C. 7–8
Smith, Adam 130
Smith, Vernon 158
social contract 15, 30, 36, 37, 45–50, 50–1, 52–6, 56, 59–61, 83–6, 96–8, 103, 105–9, 111, 116–17, 119, 121–9, 131, 151–5
space program (USA) 76–7
state of nature 29, 30, 32, 36, 46–50, 50–1, 83, 86, 126, 129, 152–3
Stubblebine, Craig 21
student protests in 1960s 25–7

taxation 16, 44–6, 64, 74, 76–7, 84, 87–8, 100, 109, 122, 126–9, 159, 162–3
  earmarked taxation 76, 113–16, 117
  just taxation 12–15, 18, 110–19
  proportional (flat) tax 118–19
  taxpayer revolts 112
Tiebout, Charles 122
Tollison, Robert 21
transitive/intransitive preferences 43, 73–5, 81, 150

Tullock, Gordon 2, 20–2, 24, 27, 28, 29, 30, 37, 42, 49, 57, 58, 66, 67, 72, 73, 74, 80, 81, 85, 88–9, 92, 94, 120–1, 130–1, 135, 137, 139, 145, 146, 147–8, 156, 158

Udehn, Lars 3, 141–4, 155
unanimity 14, 37, 54, 57–9, 85, 151–5
uncertainty 9, 72–5, 111, 114, 131, 136
  in constitutional choice 55–6
Universidad Francisco Marroquín, Guatemala 157
University of California at Los Angeles (UCLA) 24–7
University of Chicago 3, 7–16, 19–20 *see also* Chicago public choice
University of Tennessee at Knoxville 6, 8, 16
University of Turku, Finland 157

Vanberg, Viktor J. 69–71, 158
Vaughn, Karen I. 31
Vietnam War 25
Viner, Jacob 9
Virginia political economy 4, 19–32, 160
  Center for Study of Public Choice, Blacksburg, Virginia Polytechnic Institute 27–32, 157

Virginia political economy (*Cont'd*)
  Center for Study of Public Choice, Fairfax, George Mason University 31–2, 159
  Thomas Jefferson Center, Charlottesville, University of Viriginia 20–4, 28, 29, 31, 157
voting 2, 14, 17, 22, 58–9, 65–7, 74, 76–81, 82–3, 85–90, 98, 100, 102, 120–1, 131, 137, 147–8, 156, 164
  declining voter turnout 163

qualified majority
  voting 14, 58, 59, 66–7, 90, 109, 119–21
vote-trading 22, 131
see also collective choices

Wagner, Richard 21, 158
Weimar Republic (Germany) 109
welfare state 86–7, 132, 148
Wicksell, Knut 3, 11–16, 18, 19, 34, 53, 57

Yeager, Leland 21

www.ingramcontent.com/pod-product-compliance
Lightning Source LLC
Chambersburg PA
CBHW052122300426
44116CB00010B/1766